The Year of Letting Go

Also by r.h. Sin

The Year of Letting Go

365 DAYS PURSUING EMOTIONAL FREEDOM

r.h. Sin

Andrews McMeel
PUBLISHING®

Andrews McMeel Publishing
a division of Andrews McMeel Universal
1130 Walnut Street, Kansas City, Missouri 64106
www.andrewsmcmeel.com

24 25 26 27 28 SDB 10 9 8 7 6 5 4 3 2 1

ISBN: 978-1-5248-8923-4

Library of Congress Control Number: 2024933962

Editor: Patty Rice
Art Director: Diane Marsh
Production Editor: Elizabeth A. Garcia
Production Manager: Shona Burns

INTRODUCTION

Within these pages lies a journey—a daily commitment to release what weighs you down and embrace the lightness of being. Each day of the year is an opportunity to explore a new facet of letting go, through carefully selected quotes and insightful summaries that serve as your daily dose of encouragement and reflection.

This book is born from the understanding that letting go is not a one-time act but a continuous process. It's about releasing the grip on our past, our fears, our expectations, and the myriad of things that hold us back from true peace and happiness. Whether you're looking to let go of stress, past hurts, or the pressure of perfection, this guide is your companion on the path to liberation.

Each entry has been thoughtfully curated to inspire, challenge, and support you. Each quote offers a unique perspective on the art of letting go. The summaries provide context and guidance, turning each quote into a practical lesson for the day.

As you embark on this yearlong journey, remember that letting go is not about losing part of yourself but about coming back to your true essence. It's about making space for new growth, opportunities, and joy. This book is not just to be read but to be lived—one day at a time. Let it be a tool for transformation, a daily reminder that the act of letting go is, in itself, an act of immense courage and love.

JANUARY 1

"You never realized how powerful you were until you had to learn to survive a relationship that felt more like hell. And no matter how hard it got, you continued to find ways to save yourself."

There was a time when you didn't know how strong and resilient you were on the inside. You had always lived your life, going through the usual ups and downs, but you had never really been put to the test. That is, until you got into a relationship that felt more like a never-ending nightmare than a loving partnership.

The relationship started out like any other, with a sweet honeymoon phase when everything seemed perfect. But, as time went on, the cracks started to appear, showing what your relationship was really like. The relationship, which used to be healthy, turned into a toxic, all-consuming mess that made you feel stuck and suffocated. Love that used to burn so brightly was now like a roaring fire that burned everything in its way.

As the situation got worse, you wanted to get away from it more and more. The problems you were facing seemed impossible to solve, and sometimes it felt like you were stuck in hell. But through the sadness, you found something amazing in yourself: a strong, stubborn spirit that wouldn't give up.

You started to fight for your own safety by taking small but important steps to get your life back on track. You asked your friends and family for help, put your trust in them, and found comfort in what they said. You learned about the warning signs of toxic relationships and made plans to protect yourself based on what you learned.

As the days turned into weeks and months, you continued to adapt and learn, using all of your inner strength to stay afloat. No matter how many bad things happened to you, you never gave up. Instead, you saw each problem as a chance to learn, which helped you grow and become more determined.

The process was hard and painful, but every day you found new ways to save yourself. You learned how to set limits and put your own needs first. You accepted your flaws and mistakes because you knew they were a part of what made you great. Most importantly, you found out how much power you have inside you. This power had been sleeping, waiting for the right time to come out.

In the end, you rose like a phoenix from the ashes of that terrible relationship. Even though you may still have scars from your past, they are now a sign of how strong you are and a memory of how much you can grow and change. You didn't know how strong you were until you had to figure out how to get through a relationship that felt more like hell, but, now that you do, there's nothing that can stop you from continuing to rise above and overcome whatever life throws at you.

Moving on and letting go is a process; it's a decision you make each and every day. Moving on is a day-by-day line of action, and with each passing moment of choosing yourself, you look back to find that you've put more and more distance between yourself and the person who broke your heart. Each moment of every day is a journey on a path that will not only put distance between you and everything that caused you pain but will also inform you of what to do moving forward as you continue to heal and cultivate joy.

JANUARY 2

"Stop making the wrong people feel special. No matter how hard you try, they'll never be right for you."

The realization that you are wasting your time on someone who doesn't deserve it is vital to your peace of mind and the health of your future. No matter how hard you try, this kind of person will never really recognize or return your kindness. Turn your attention to building relationships with people who care about and respect you. These relationships will help you grow and be happy. Keep an eye out for signs that someone isn't right for you, and don't be afraid to set limits to protect your mental health and overall well-being. It's important to put your own needs first and entertain people who care about you. By doing this, you will create a loving and helpful setting that will make your life better.

JANUARY 3

"It's tough, but the reward in walking away is more peace and the opportunity to find the person who has been searching for someone like you."

It can be hard to leave a bad relationship, but doing so can lead to a happier life and help you meet people with better intentions. As you put yourself first and free yourself from the responsibilities of maintaining an unhealthy relationship, you make room in your life for someone who will really love and appreciate all the unique things about you and everything you have to offer. By valuing yourself and accepting your own worth, you become a beacon of energy for those who are looking for someone like you.

The time you spend alone serves as a reminder that you are fully capable of cultivating the joy and peace you have always felt you deserved even in the absence of others, which itself is a true strength. And from there, you begin to understand the value in sharing what you've built with someone who wants to protect and support that foundation. Someone who is willing and ready to add to what you've built.

JANUARY 4

"Sometimes, we give them too much credit. Sometimes, we overexaggerate their power. Sometimes, they don't really break you; maybe you simply break yourself by trying to hold on to them."

Sometimes, we give destructive people in our lives way too much power over our emotions. By doing this, we might make their effect on us greater than it would have been if we'd set boundaries and or refused to entertain their negativity. The truth is, sometimes what makes us feel bad emotionally is our willingness to share the power to dictate our mood with people who mostly intend to hurt us. We hurt ourselves attempting to maintain relationships that are not worthy of being kept.

It's important to know when to let go and when to remove ourselves from situations that will only distract us from the life and love we long for. You set the standard for how you'd want to be treated by setting boundaries, thus creating a greater possibility of receiving the treatment you know your heart deserves.

JANUARY 5

"It's fucked up that you had to learn about love from those who never loved you."

Those first experiences with an emotion so profound such as love can also be some of the most hurtful moments in one's life. Too often, the people who make us feel like we're in love are also the same individuals who force us into feelings of anguish and loneliness. You quickly learn how rare genuine love is as you enter relationship after relationship. You soon realize that the love you're looking for has become a disguise for those who are looking to manipulate you into giving them a space in your heart that they do not deserve.

JANUARY 6

"You deserve something you don't have to question; you deserve someone who is sure about you."

You should feel valued, appreciated, and sure of your partner's commitment to the relationship. Trust, mutual respect, and open conversation are all vital and important when attempting to form the foundation that will help a relationship grow and sustain itself, allowing both people to feel safe, cared for, and understood in the best ways possible. You shouldn't have to spend the majority of your relationship floating in limbo, asking yourself what your place is in the relationship and or how that person actually feels about you.

When you're with someone who is sure about you, you can work together to grow and get through life's problems. It's important to know how much you're worth and not settle for anything less than total love and support.

In the end, having a relationship with someone who is sure of how they feel about you can bring you more emotional satisfaction; happiness that lasts; and a positive, profound effect on your overall mental health.

JANUARY 7

"When the past is better than the
present, there is no future."

Most relationships begin in bloom from the seed of potential, but just like a dream that transforms into a nightmare, the beginning is beautiful. So much so that the terror that awaits can catch you off guard. This is because all of the energy of most relationships is packed into the start and fades away as time goes on. You must find a way to take the love you feel for someone and not only spread it out evenly over time but also find ways to help it grow, evolve, expand, and continuously serve as a well of care, understanding, and connection.

Knowing this, you should see no obligation to stay with someone who wants you to remain stuck in misery and heartache. The best days of your relationship should not live only in the past; the best moments of your relationship are not to be restricted to moments long gone. You can't grow in love if all the energy and devotion is no longer expressed in the present. You can't give life to the future if your relationship is strictly reliant on the good times of the past.

JANUARY 8

"Ignore the excuses; their actions are their truth."

In navigating the complexities of human interaction and interpersonal relationships, it's essential to remember this powerful piece of advice: Please, for the sake of your emotional health and peace of mind, don't get swayed by their excuses and words, because actions truly speak louder than anything that can be spoken. People often resort to beautifully formed, eloquent phrases and words, but they are all empty in meaning and are well-constructed excuses to justify their bad behavior and mistreatment or to paint a picture that might not align with what is actually going on.

If their words constantly contradict their actions, it's an undeniable sign that they are in fact not the person they promised you they'd be and that they are nowhere near becoming the person you deserve or need.

JANUARY 9

"burn bridges if you have to

don't be afraid of the flames

use the fire as warmth

use the fire as a torch

to light the path toward

something better

with someone better"

At the beginning of all relationships, roads are paved, paths are cleared and renewed, and bridges are built. Over time, those bridges can be maintained and strengthened or forced into the process of breakdown, in which they are weakened by the rust of mistrust and harsh emotional conditions.

It is then that you are faced with the choice to either continue to force yourself into the maintenance of that structure or decide that it is time for it to crumble. Or, better yet, you burn those bridges to serve as warmth or light so that you can begin working on cultivating an exit that leads you back to yourself.

January 10

"you were just an illusion

of everything

i thought i needed

you were just a lie

pretending to be the truth"

When the person you believed you needed turns out to be nothing more than an alluring illusion, the realization can be both disheartening and eye-opening. It is then when you gain a powerful lesson. No longer blinded by a lie, you are able to see a life of peace outside of the chaos of settling for the wrong person.

Those initial illusions may have been crafted by your own desires and expectations, painting a picture of the love you thought you deserved, cultivating a doctored photograph of what you wished to see instead of the actual events in the frame. However, as the veil lifts, you come to understand that what you perceived as love was merely an enchanting and beautiful lie.

It is a moment of reckoning, where you confront the stark disparity between your idealized vision and the reality of what sits before you. This realization may bring a sense of disappointment and sadness, but it also presents an opportunity to discover that you alone are more than enough. Through this experience, you learn to discern genuine love from fleeting illusions, and from this, you create a new path that isn't littered with distractions and more of what you should avoid in your search for something real.

JANUARY 11

"sometimes, sadness

is the only way out

painful is the path

that leads

to something better"

S adness is sometimes the only way to get away from the chaos
and confusion of life. Sadness is understanding of all things and
events that wish to bring you further pain and anguish. Sadness is like
a key that locks a door made of material that is best at keeping out
what should no longer be allowed in.

Healing is often a long and hard process, with hearts that hurt
and trails that are stained with tears. But even in the worst parts
of this painful road, there is hope for something better. Through
suffering, we learn to be strong and find the strength to start over. We
find the seeds of change in the world of sadness and carefully care for
them until they grow into a better tomorrow.

January 12

"Your ex was just an exaggeration of what you thought you needed."

Before we even meet a person, we cultivate dreams of what we want our relationship to be. Unknowingly, we project those dreams and expectations onto the person we decide to be with, and it is often in the end that we come to this realization that the person we want to be with is not the same person we need to be with.

When you focus on what you dream that person to be, you ignore the nightmare they've become. It's time to wake up to the reality of heartache so that you can truly begin the journey of healing and self-love.

JANUARY 13

"Sometimes, you have to lose what you want to get what you need."

You walk into a relationship because you want to cultivate and nurture a love for another person, and sometimes it takes being with the wrong person to understand what it is you truly need.

I've been where you are, struggling with the realization that the person you want to be with is not the same person you need. Even when you try to force it, somewhere along the way, the person you're fighting for just stops showing up, and it is then when you discover that you can't create a harmonious relationship with someone you can't rely on. This is when you learn the difference between your wants and needs. If you focus on what you need, you'll realize that you were just settling.

JANUARY 14

"Stop planting yourself in dead gardens."

It can be tempting to stay in a relationship that doesn't nurture you in a way that helps you bloom. Sometimes, we hold on for far too long because of time invested, but no amount of time and care can help one grow in soil that has been tainted with lies and betrayal.

JANUARY 15

"Leave and they'll search for you in everyone else and fail. This is when they'll understand what they lost."

There's just something rare inside you, something genuinely authentic in the way you care and love others, especially the person you give your heart to. It's just that sometimes a star is not appreciated until it is nowhere to be found in the night sky. It is in that profound realization, that striking moment of clarity, that they will comprehend the magnitude of what they have lost in their attempt to break your heart and abandon you.

The absence of your presence will become a void they can never fill, and they will yearn for the depth of connection they once shared with you and that energy you once willingly gave freely without limitations. The lesson will be learned, albeit too late, that losing someone extraordinary is an irreparable loss that no substitute can heal.

JANUARY 16

"i later learned

to appreciate the absence

of those who failed to

cherish my presence

alone, through self-discovery

i learned to love myself

even the parts of my soul

that were often overlooked

and taken for granted"

So many of us fear the loneliness that occupies our hearts once a relationship is over, but we also forget that there was loneliness sitting in our chests even while in that relationship. You're not supposed to be alone when you're with someone. Being in a relationship should not force you into a corner of regret, sadness, and depression. And so, it is only fitting that you rediscover the power of solitude and the gift that is being alone with the only person who matters, the only person capable of providing the love you need the most: yourself.

You alone are worthy of your heart, dedication, and time. You alone are fully capable of providing yourself with all the things that were kept from you in your previous relationship. You will find that a better relationship with yourself is not only healing but it will open the right doors to the right person. Someone capable of matching the same energy you are now free to give yourself. Someone with pieces that fit the missing parts and empty parts of yourself. Understand that you will not be starved when alone because you are capable of feeding yourself. Understand that you alone are also the love of your life and that in being single you have the precious opportunity to practice in the type of self-love that will help define the type of love you accept from others.

JANUARY 17

"The greatest pain produces the strongest hearts."

Intense suffering can often produce the most courageous people. Our characters are strengthened by the suffering of being with the wrong people, and while each unhealthy relationship may leave a scar or two, our hearts gain pearls of wisdom that make them that much harder to break. In the midst of suffering, we find our strongest reserves of fortitude and muster up the willpower to move forth despite our overwhelming feelings of hopelessness. The suffering and the sadness that follows makes us more resilient. Our hearts are strengthened by the wounds of our past, and through these experiences, we learn lessons of survival. Even in the face of overwhelming stress and adversity, we find the fortitude to persevere and grow from the depths of heartbreak.

January 18

"A relationship without loyalty is like a body with no soul. A relationship without loyalty crumbles the bridge between two lovers."

L oyalty is a bridge between two lovers, a bridge that can be immediately torn down in the face of betrayal. The ability to remain faithful to your beloved is a way to express how important you view not only the relationship but how much you value the person who trusts you.

In the wake of deception, you learn how quickly that trust can be destroyed and how a bridge that once appeared indestructible now struggles to remain whole. Loyalty informs strength and vulnerability. Loyalty is the lifeblood of the relationship, and without it, there is no soul and no reason to go on.

JANUARY 19

"You are not difficult to love. Your soul mate will love you with ease."

It is easy to believe in the difficulty of love when you're with the wrong person. It is easy to believe that what you're looking for doesn't exist when the person you have fallen for isn't capable of matching your effort and energy. We sometimes define love by people who don't genuinely love us back, and as we accept their lack of effort, we begin to blame ourselves, weighed down by this idea that maybe we are, in fact, too hard to love.

This is not the case; you can't blame yourself for someone's inability to love you in the way you need. Here's the thing: It's not going to be easy. The path that will lead you to healthy love will be littered with many things you don't want from many people who will make false claims of love. But as you've been with the wrong person, you gain an understanding of what to trust and who to avoid.

Finding the right partner is not about discovering perfection. It's about finding someone who cares for you enough to match what you offer in a relationship. Finding the right partner is about discovering someone who allows you the freedom to feel safe and to be vulnerable as you both cultivate spaces where love can bloom.

January 20

"The broken can be beautiful; you are proof of this."

Like stars in the shade of midnight, you find ways to explore your brightest light during your darkest hours. You turn rainstorms into moments of growth and heartache into lessons of what and who not to love. You may feel broken now, but broken is where you begin again. Broken is where you rebuild again.

JANUARY 21

"People leave too soon; feelings stay too long."

Sometimes, the feelings linger around longer than the people you feel things for. It can be maddening, chaotic, and senseless, but at least you know that these feelings are unconditional and genuine. At times, when you feel stuck in an emotion you no longer wish to feel, it just means that what you felt for that person was real.

January 22

"Being single could be the beginning
of something better than what
you've had."

When a relationship ends, we're overcome with fear and sadness, but what we tend to forget is the only reason that relationship began was that you were in a position of loneliness; it started from the path of being single. And the end just places you back in a place where a new journey can begin.

JANUARY 23

"Maybe there's never room for something new or something better because you're always holding on to things that no longer deserve to take up space."

Remember this and carry this mindset wherever you go, especially as you find yourself in a relationship that is unhealthy or find yourself struggling with the urge to go back to a place that is no longer worthy of your energy and time: You will never find better, settling for something or someone who is content with behavior that breaks your heart.

Some people struggle with leaving, while others struggle with not going back. You can't cultivate self-love while wasting that love on someone who no longer appreciates you, and you'll never discover the joy of a healthy relationship if you can't get past a relationship that has no future.

January 24

"Perhaps you left because I
deserved more."

Rightfully so, you take the perspective of the abandoned when someone walks out of your life, but even in your sadness, I hope you understand that sometimes people walk away because they themselves understand that they are not worthy of all the things you have to offer. Sometimes, you lose people because they can't keep up with you. Sometimes, you lose a person because they realize that they are incapable of matching your energy. And so, instead of remaining in a picture that will never fit the frame, they leave, denying the challenge of being better.

You can't force a person to be who they are not ready to be, even if that person made promises to become that one day.

JANUARY 25

"Being single is a time to heal."

Being single is a transition into the process of healing. That moment between the end of a relationship and the beginning of another is a chance to rediscover yourself, your strengths, and your ability to comprehend the lessons given to you from every relationship that doesn't last.

When you are single, you are free to pour everything that was taken for granted into yourself. The time you once shared with someone else now belongs to you. Being single is a space of creation, an opportunity to rebuild your self-esteem and confidence. And I know it isn't easy, but be patient with yourself. Feel everything you need to feel so that you can begin to appreciate this newly discovered solitude.

JANUARY 26

"you are alone

in need of more of yourself"

The days turn to weeks, the weeks become months, and one day you wake up to the realization that sometimes a relationship needs to end so that you can get closer to yourself.

The season of heartbreak is filled with profound lessons about who you are and what to do as far as moving forward with your life. When the dust settles, you are enlightened by the fractures in your heart.

Being in the wrong relationship causes one to lose themselves, their identity lost to the effort and time invested in trying to be someone others can love instead of becoming more of who they're meant to be. And when a relationship ends, there's a sufficient amount of time granted to the possibilities of finding real love within your own heart. You are alone right now so that you can practice a love for yourself and a passion that you've struggled to find in others.

JANUARY 27

"Leave the past in the past. The strongest fires can't be cultivated with old flames."

The thinking here is that you shouldn't attempt to rebuild your happiness and peace with the same materials and tools that forced you to lose everything you valued and or that made you feel as if you had to compromise the things you needed just to be with someone who, in the end, didn't genuinely want you.

How can you cultivate a strong relationship with someone too weak to fight the temptation to hurt you? How is a healthy relationship possible with someone who doesn't see the need to change their toxic ways? Nothing beautiful can be made with someone who is comfortable with making you feel ugly inside.

JANUARY 28

"You were a nightmare wrapped
in something beautiful. A disaster,
presented as a gift."

I sn't that how it often happens? In your time of need and in the last
hour of your emptiness, someone walks into your life resembling
everything you've dreamed of, saying all the things you never thought
you'd hear. That dream stands in front of you, and a beautiful future
feels like the promise, but after some time, you are unable to remain
blind to the truth, and what once felt like salvation has become your
own personal hell.

When you've gone without love for too long, when you're weary
from the weight of loneliness, it's so easy to believe in a lie, and the
devil always has the best timing for people who would do anything to
feel loved once more.

January 29

"Sometimes, crying means letting go. Sometimes, the only way to empty yourself of a person is to cry them out of your heart."

The act of crying is often associated with weakness, but that idea is all wrong. Crying is a riverway to an ocean of freedom. Crying is an attempt at releasing the things that are causing pain, the things that are keeping you stuck in the pits of heartbreak.

When you cry, you distance yourself from all the things that do not deserve to keep you from experiencing peace and joy. When you cry, you are strengthening your heart to go on without the things you thought you needed and the people you thought would always love you.

JANUARY 30

"Overwhelmed by a sea of emotions, sometimes you have to drown to learn how to swim."

You didn't know your strengths until you were forced into the act of being strong. You didn't know how brave you were until you were faced with an ending that caused you to dig deep in search of the courage to go on. Sometimes, the things that break you help you learn how to piece it all back together again.

These moments can be overwhelming at first, and the lessons that live in your darkest hours are often hard to comprehend, but with time, I hope you find the gift beyond this pain.

JANUARY 31

"We try our hardest to force life into things that must die, and that's what hurts the most."

It's so hard to leave when you're too busy investing your energy into trying to rescue something unsavable.

We hurt ourselves unnecessarily trying to breathe life into a ghost of everything that could have been. Overthinking ourselves into what-if scenarios. Blaming ourselves for someone else's decisions when in reality you did everything you could do. But none of it will ever be good enough for someone who isn't good enough for you.

FEBRUARY 1

"The path to self-love is paved
with self-acceptance, forgiveness,
and growth."

S elf-love is protection; self-love is a guard dog for your heart. The path to great self-love is a tough one, filled with dead ends and wrong exits, but all in all, it is a necessary road to take.

Forgive yourself for choosing the wrong person. It happens. Forgive yourself for wanting to go backward. That also happens; it's normal. Accept that you are not perfect; accept the fact that you are not free of mistakes and judgment rooted directly in emotion. From forgiveness and self-acceptance, you allow yourself a chance to grow, and in your growth, you blossom into someone who is capable of moving forward even when it may feel impossible.

The Year of Letting Go

FEBRUARY 2

"A heart that forgives is a heart that heals."

The longer you hold out on forgiveness, the further you are from truly letting go. Every so often, you will discover that, in this life, you may have to forgive people who were never genuinely sorry for the terrible things they did, but in doing so, you make the process of letting go that much easier. And with that, you welcome internal and emotional healing.

FEBRUARY 3

"In nurturing self-love, we become
beacons of immersive light that
attract real love to our shores."

No one ever really tells you this from the beginning, but
sometimes you attract what you genuinely feel. I think it's
important to know that people who wish to take advantage of others
can usually spot the emptiness and the sadness that comes with a lack
of self-love or overall self-esteem. On the other hand, self-love can
also be seen and observed by the same people who would otherwise
attempt to use or take advantage of you, and it repels them, as it acts
as a warning and indication that you are more likely to demand what
you need and are less likely to put up with toxic individuals.

When you love yourself, you set the ultimate example for how
you are to be loved by others. Self-love attracts the right love because
it helps you produce this beautiful inner light that can only be seen
by those who will appreciate it.

FEBRUARY 4

"Endings can be painful, but new beginnings carry the promise of a beautiful start, surrounded by all the things that deserve your presence, care, and attention."

I can recall a time when I was faced with the ending of a relationship that I believed would last, dread, doom, and gloom. It felt tragic, as most breakups do, but then you're forced to dwell in the ending; you take up residence there with no choice but to reevaluate everything that has happened and begin to set in motion everything that will. With time, you figure out how to transform that breakup into a breakthrough, a greater understanding of what you need and how to tell the difference between healthy and toxic bonds.

FEBRUARY 5

"Change is a revelation that paves the way toward self-discovery and peace of mind. Embrace it."

Any type of change can be scary; it forces you to walk a path that is uncertain, unfamiliar, and uncomfortable, but if you want to experience something that is different from what you've faced in the past, you have to take an alternate route, and, more times than not, it is the disappointment and or betrayal from someone whom you cared for that pushes you to take that risk.

Some of you will fight it, and some will give in a little faster than others, but the most important thing to understand is that it will happen on your time and when you are ready. It will happen because it has, and you have always been able to do what is necessary to get what you need.

FEBRUARY 6

"I'm always okay, no matter what. This is what I've come to realize: that at every ending, there is always a space provided to me for a new beginning."

Something better always waits for me, and the day that isn't the case will be the moment of me discovering where I belong; there's a part of me, the biggest part of me, that looks forward to that day.

I can remember being young and fearful of the end, afraid of starting over, but the painful experiences of being hurt by those I've trusted helped me understand that, in order to gain more, in order to gain better, I must lose what should not be held on to.

February 7

"Every loss brings you closer to what
deserves to be kept."

What you initially believe is a failure is really just another step on the stairway leading up to everything you deserve. Today, reflect on the idea that every time you thought you were losing something, you were really gaining the opportunity to have more, to have better.

FEBRUARY 8

"Just because you have the emotional range and strength to love a shit person doesn't mean you should."

Remember, sometimes strength is not about how easy it is to hold on but how you handle the difficulty of letting go. The stronger you are, the more you feel you should tolerate. You think that because your heart is capable of withstanding great amounts of damage, you should settle or give multiple chances to someone who never deserved the first one. Just because you can handle it doesn't mean you should accept it.

February 9

"Running from the heartache just
makes it hurt even more once it
catches up to you."

Have you ever attempted to avoid a certain thought, only for
that thought to grow larger in your mind the more you focus
on ignoring it. That same thing happens when you attempt to avoid
the pain that is naturally felt when things don't go the way you've
planned. Face the things that are bothering you so that you don't have
to expend any energy on them later.

FEBRUARY 10

"You leave before you get left. You want love, but you're afraid of getting hurt."

You're not alone in this feeling. I, too, have felt this way in the past. Sometimes, we self-sabotage something that could be good because of all the bad experiences we've had in the past. The key is self-love and understanding. Don't let what lies behind you dictate the direction of where you're headed. Don't let bad experiences keep you from discovering everything you've missed in your last relationship.

February 11

"It takes time to detach from the
wrong people because, at one time,
you believed them all to be worthy of
being kept."

Take your time as you move closer to healing, but don't give too
much energy to the thought of someone who refused to invest
the same mental energy into the relationship. Never rush the healing
process, but never stay too long in a place that doesn't serve you.

FEBRUARY 12

"The more you love yourself, the less you're willing to tolerate being in a relationship with someone who acts as if they hate you."

Self-love acts as protection against further damage from those who have proven unworthy of your time and energy. When you love yourself, you send out a signal to those with bad intentions that you are not willing to put up with their nonsense and mistreatment.

FEBRUARY 13

"You can feel anything you want today.

Choose peace; choose joy."

P eace is a decision; joy is a choice. When you realize that you alone have the ability to move from rain clouds to the sun, you begin to restrict access to your heart from the people who often push you to a place of negative emotions. Today and every day after, you must try your hardest to choose yourself and do what's in your best interest so that you no longer remain a prisoner to feelings caused by people who do not care about you.

FEBRUARY 14

"I hope something undeniably good happens to you because you are deserving of something beautiful after all the shit you've been through."

Sometimes, we think ourselves into a corner of loneliness. Sadness begins to overrun our future, spilling out from our past. We begin to believe that we will never find love because every road we've taken often feels like a dead end, but in the aftermath of whatever destruction has found your heart, in the aftermath of the storm clouds that produced heavy rain that may have drowned out so much of the hope you've clung to, there is still something left. There is still a road to take, a path that can only be discovered in the end of what no longer should continue. There is still love in your heart, and I hope you find yourself. And when you do, I hope something good finds you, like the movement of the ocean to the shore.

FEBRUARY 15

"Their mixed signals are screaming 'no.'
Please stay away from anyone who is
confused about what they feel for you."

Mixed signals are the enemy of the certainty of love. When someone appears to be uncertain about the way they feel about you, their actions toward you provoke a battle from within that can often lower self-esteem or, even worse, diminish the level of courage needed to walk away from that relationship. Don't be afraid to leave behind a person who isn't afraid to lose you.

February 16

"It is only when you distance yourself from certain people that you know when to stay and when to leave."

Take a step back. Sometimes, the truth is harder to comprehend when you're standing too close to a relationship that has caused you to question whether or not you should stay or go. Some distance will help you understand that maybe it is in your best interest to move further away rather than force yourself closer into oblivion.

February 17

"You can't be cured by the person who
chooses to poison your heart."

E very so often, we find ourselves reaching for the hands of the
people who are the reason for our trauma. Understand that you
can't get well with the person who makes your heart sick.

FEBRUARY 18

"Anyone who wants you to be anything but happy is not worthy of your fucking time."

Either surround yourself with people who make you feel the right things or just learn to find solace in your own company. It doesn't make sense to attempt to fill your life with people who cause you to feel empty. In most cases, you are all that you need. Learn to celebrate your ability to provide your own heart with everything it has lost to the hands of those who were not brave enough to care for it. In every day, make your happiness a priority and understand that the more you let go, the closer you'll be to all the things you were distracted from by lovers who couldn't love you.

FEBRUARY 19

"Look into the mirror. Some see
a reflection, while others see a
soul mate."

Looking into the mirror creates a profound encounter with your true essence. While you may feel broken, tired, and confused, when you look into the mirror, don't just see someone worth saving; also see someone capable of saving themselves.

FEBRUARY 20

"It's time to stop missing people who forget about you so easily."

It's okay to feel the hurt; it proves that you cared. But, remember, your pain is not your identity; your pain doesn't define who you are. You are more than the heartache, stronger than the sorrow. Let the tears cleanse your heart, making room for the healing to come.

FEBRUARY 21

"You can miss someone and still
change the locks to your heart."

When you genuinely care for someone, the love you show
them is unconditional, and so when you are faced with the
decision to walk away, leaving is difficult because it was never a part
of the plan. You move forward because you know that, in order to
live a healthy life, you have to purge the things that keep you sick,
but every now and then, especially when the wounds are fresh, you
are allowed space to miss the person you thought they were while
accepting the truth in who they are.

February 22

"Love isn't just about finding the right person, and I think the search gets talked about so often that sometimes we forget that it's also about being the right person."

Today, set the standard for the love you want by being the person your heart needs. In being single, you are provided a canvas to illustrate the type of person you wish to love by simply loving yourself.

FEBRUARY 23

"Breakups are not failures but opportunities to learn and grow."

In this life, you'll find that we mostly learn from the things that don't work out. I like to think that when you begin to heal after heartbreak, there's a form presented to you, a sort of questionnaire and a bit of note-taking that you subconsciously did while in that relationship and in the spaces between the breakup and finding someone new. There is a list of things that you learned from the person who ultimately let you down, or maybe it's the other way around and what you see is a list of mistakes that you will work toward not repeating in your next relationship.

FEBRUARY 24

"Time heals; let it."

I think we're always rushing toward something to take the pain away without fully understanding that being present; being honest about the feeling, no matter how difficult or tragic it may be; and confronting it all head-on without a helmet or a shield is where healing can begin. It's the moment when the tears overflow so much that they burn your eyes or your voice loses its strength, fading behind the cracking of your aching heart. In your darkest hour, if you stand outside, beneath a night sky, free of shade, you will welcome the healing powers that live within you. Take your time.

FEBRUARY 25

"The end of a relationship isn't the end
of your life."

When breakups happen, it's easy to lose sight of your worth.
Don't let a love lost make you feel less than you've always
been. You are valuable, unique, and deserving of true happiness.
Remind yourself of this every day.

FEBRUARY 26

"Don't lose yourself in a relationship;

stay true to who you are."

U nderstand that being with the right person doesn't require you to compromise yourself and your needs. Staying true to yourself in the season of being single will also attract a relationship in which you don't have to fight who you're with about who you are.

FEBRUARY 27

"Find someone who inspires you, not
intimidates you."

The partner you ultimately choose to be with should inspire
whatever is within you to expand and evolve. The person you
share your heart with should help it feel safe, and their actions should
motivate your feelings of love to not only grow toward that person
but also be turned inward. When you love the right person, they
don't seek to intimidate and or manipulate you. When your love of
self is able to exist fully with the love you have for someone else, only
then have you found true love.

February 28

"Don't let past relationships dictate the present relationship you have with yourself."

We often fear the unknown, the void that a relationship leaves behind. However, within that void lies the untapped potential for something better, something worthy of our attention. It's an open space for personal growth, for rediscovery, for new love. Embrace the unknown, for it is the birthplace of everything you've dreamed of.

MARCH 1

"Build a relationship; don't just fall into one."

The relationships that don't last are all filled with information on how to properly cultivate a relationship that stands a chance. So often, we fall into a relationship with no clue of what to do to maintain it. Think back on the things that went wrong, and spend a moment to make a mental list of what could have been done to make the outcome much different or what it is you need in order to feel at home in your relationship. All of these things, luckily, can be practiced when you're single and on your own. Create the standard, create boundaries, and a list of do's and don'ts. Think back on what hurt you so that you can avoid repeating the same pain over and over again.

MARCH 2

"Remember, affection is more than just words."

Stop making room in your mind for people who rarely think about you. Stop making room in your heart for people who make you feel like you are not deserving of love. Stop making room for people who refuse to provide room for you. Stop making room for people who do not provide a space for love, truth, and commitment.

MARCH 3

"Sometimes, love means letting go."

Sometimes, the easiest way to practice self-love is in the act of letting go of someone else, especially if that person isn't ready to love you in the way you need. Just as it is an act of self-love, it is also an expression of genuine love toward the person you are leaving behind because you are leaving them and making space for the right person to enter their lives as well.

MARCH 4

"You can't force someone to realize that you're what's best for them."

You can be good to someone, and you can be the best thing in their lives, but you can't force a person to see you as more than they're willing to comprehend. And it's not your job to convince someone that loving you is a beautiful choice to make, and it's okay to walk away and preserve yourself for someone who will.

MARCH 5

"Nothing about the future can be
beautiful if you're focused on the past."

The more you dwell in the past, the greater your absence in the present, and the stronger the impossibilities become for the future. You can't water the garden of your future if you're fixed upon the dead roots of your past.

MARCH 6

"Do not overthink yourself back into the wrong relationship."

J ust because it's the wrong relationship doesn't mean it's easy to leave behind. Oftentimes, one of the reasons why people struggle to let go is because they overthink themselves back into committing a pattern that is self-destructive and that obstructs their view of something better. The moments after a breakup are the hardest because you literally think up scenarios where things go differently, where things work out even when it's just not in the cards to turn out the way you initially hoped. Don't spend your days hoping for something that won't happen, and do not give your nights to someone who no longer thinks of you in a way that inspires them to treat you with kindness and respect. It's time to see that relationship for what it was: just a lesson. Nothing more.

MARCH 7

"You are more, and you deserve more
than what they are willing to give you."

S ay it with me: "Settling is the enemy of genuine love." Say it
again, but this time with your eyes closed. It happens sometimes.
You enter a relationship with someone whose intentions don't match
yours, and over the duration of that relationship, you discover that
what you are getting just doesn't match up with the love you believe
in your heart you deserve. Settling is the enemy of the future you
could have and the love you could have when you refuse to settle.

MARCH 8

"You can forgive people, but you don't
have to give them second chances."

Forgiveness doesn't have to be a way back in. Forgiving someone allows you to move past them. Don't let anyone force you to believe that in order to resolve your feelings, you have to allow them back into your life. Forgiveness is kindness turned inward.

MARCH 9

"You have been strong for so long. Cry
if you need to; scream if it helps."

Face what you feel so that you no longer have to be imprisoned by
it. Crying is not a weakness; it is a route taken by the things that
no longer need to be carried around in the heart. Crying is how we
release what no longer deserves to take up residence in the heart.

MARCH 10

"Sometimes, the love you crave can't be found in the person you want."

It's a hard truth to accept, but sometimes we want the wrong things with the best intentions, and there will be times in our lives when we love a thing that doesn't appreciate it. When you are ready to face the fact that what you love is keeping you from finding love, then you are ready to enter a pathway of self-love and healing.

MARCH 11

"Loving someone is not a reason to allow them chances to continuously break your heart."

L ove is not to be used as an excuse to allow mistreatment. Do not taint the true meaning of love just to be with someone who provides a false sense of what it actually is.

MARCH 12

"Missing that person doesn't mean you're weak. It means you're strong enough to remain honest in your emotional truth."

It's okay to miss someone while being faced with the understanding that you shouldn't go back there. It may seem counterproductive at times, but in remembering where you were, you also remember why it is you left in the first place.

MARCH 13

"Falling for someone doesn't mean they'll catch you. Loving someone doesn't make them deserve you."

Love is never enough for a person who doesn't love themselves enough to allow genuine love in from others. Love will never be enough for the person you're not supposed to be with. Love will never be enough for a relationship that isn't meant to work out. Just because you love someone doesn't mean they will or have to love you in return. Love should never feel forced, and it does nothing to force that love into hands that will never cherish it.

MARCH 14

"There's still magic in a heart that's been broken."

Breakups can feel like heavy storms, but even storms have purpose. They water the earth, encouraging growth and evolution. In the same way, let this difficult time be your nourishing rain. May you grow stronger, wiser, and more resilient because of this heartbreak.

March 15

"You are not your past. Be here, be present, be more."

You might be feeling like you've lost a part of yourself, but don't forget the rest of you that's still whole. Take this opportunity to reacquaint yourself with who you've always been and who you are in the aftermath of this pain. In your journey to find yourself again, you might just discover something even more beautiful.

MARCH 16

"Since the beginning, you have always been more than enough."

You have always been more than enough, with or without a relationship. You enter this endless cycle of thinking the person you're with will define the amount of love you will receive and or deserve, but this, in truth, isn't the case. Remember that, in every moment of your life, you are capable of giving yourself the greatest love and that your heart remains valuable even when it isn't in the hands of someone else.

MARCH 17

"Today, I need you to know that you
will outgrow the sorrows that plague
your soul and you will find the
happiness you've always needed right
there in the core of your own heart..."

You're tired of running away from everything that hurts. You're weary because of the restless nights when sleep is all you want, but sleep is the hardest thing to find. I need you to understand that everything you're feeling right now is necessary on your path toward healing. The more you face what you feel, the closer you are to overcoming these daily battles that seemingly break your heart. The more you're honest with what your heart is actually feeling, the more you will outgrow the sadness in your heart. Sometimes, pain can be transformed into a resource that nurtures strength and wisdom. Use what you've gone through to get through this.

MARCH 18

"the moon will fade

the sun will rise

and you will learn

to let them go"

Tomorrow is another chance to set free what or who no longer wants to fight for a position in your life. Each day serves as an opportunity to set yourself free from whatever has been holding you back from the happiness you've been longing to cultivate and maintain.

MARCH 19

"You set yourself free by letting go of
anyone who wants to leave."

Remember this: a person who wants to remain in your life will
not continuously do things that cause you to question the
way they feel about you. And if the person you're with is forcing you
closer to a tough decision of whether to stay or go, understand that
this is truly a sign that you deserve more and that the only way to get
closer to that is to put distance between yourself and the person you
believed could love you.

MARCH 20

"Heartache is the price we pay for taking the risk of trusting someone enough to fall for them."

There's no real way to avoid heartbreak; of course, you can learn all that you need to learn in an effort to decrease the chances of getting hurt or to reduce the scope in which you choose the wrong person, but, ultimately, the journey that is finding the right person will be filled with misplaced love and trust.

For many of us, the journey toward lasting love will be littered with love invested in the wrong places, but that's just the price you pay to travel home.

March 21

"The end of a relationship may feel like the end of the world, but it's merely the end of a chapter in the ongoing book on the pursuit of love. Another page begins, ready to be filled with new experiences and lessons."

The end is simply the place where you will learn how to begin again. Once you enter the world of relationships, you're forced to learn quickly that life is filled with endings and that, somehow or someway, you unconsciously fight your way toward a new beginning. This is what you've done, what you do, and what you will always be capable of. When you're ready, think back on all the times you found the will to begin again, then do it.

MARCH 22

"The pain of letting go is only temporary, and the pain of holding on for too long can be endless."

It's a strange thing, deciding to stay in a space that makes us feel everything we don't want; the fear of letting go stems from the perceived idea of forever loneliness, and yet the very thing keeping us constantly facing the dread of neglect is our inability to walk away. The hurt of staying with the wrong person is far greater than the pain that is felt when transitioning out of an unhealthy relationship.

March 23

"Even while our hearts may break,

they also mend in the most beautiful

of ways. With time, the cracks can

become the places where we are the

strongest."

Sometimes, the demolition of a structure occurs so that
something stronger can take its place. In so many ways, this is
what is happening to you. From ruins, the strongest version of you
will be born again.

MARCH 24

"In every ending, there's a new beginning hidden behind all of the sadness and regret. It's your job to uncover it."

Breakups can be tough, but they also mean you're free to move forward with your life and fully focus on decisions that'll shape your life in the way you deserve. Breakups are chances to learn, grow, and find someone better suited for you. Just because one chapter ends doesn't mean the whole book is over.

MARCH 25

"Moving on isn't about forgetting every painful thing that occurred; it's about learning to live with the memory without allowing it to dictate your life."

Forcing yourself to forget about all the things that went wrong keeps you stuck and renders you incapable of moving forward. It's a beautiful moment when you discover that you can live with some of the memories that hurt you and still experience joy. This is a process of healing.

MARCH 26

"The breakup isn't just about ending a relationship; it's about finding yourself again."

U ltimately, a breakup isn't completely driven by the need to get away from another person; oftentimes, it's about moving closer to yourself. The wrong relationships stand in the way of self-actualization, preventing growth, both mentally and emotionally. You leave the wrong relationship so that you can prepare a space to better your relationship with yourself.

MARCH 27

"You cannot force someone to comprehend your value or the message they're not ready to receive. Move on, grow, and wish them well as you move forward without them."

Attempting to force someone to understand your worth is a waste of a life and a detriment to the love in your heart. Your energy is better spent on personal growth and in spaces where your value is acknowledged and or appreciated. This does not mean harboring ill feelings toward the person; instead, offer them grace as they journey through their own process of understanding. The act of moving on should not be viewed as a loss but rather an opportunity to gain more of what you need as you venture out into the right direction.

MARCH 28

"Devoting yourself to someone incapable of loving you can hurt, but it also teaches us resilience."

The experience of giving love to someone who is incapable of reciprocating can be one of the most painful experiences, as it often feels like a constant struggle against their refusal to accept what you've given to them. However, this painful experience can help us cultivate resilience by forcing us to confront our deepest vulnerabilities and develop emotional strength and wisdom. It teaches us to endure and persist even when we feel like we're running on empty, cultivating a capacity for picking ourselves up whenever we've fallen for the wrong person. This is when we discover that our value is not determined by another person's inability to love us but by our own capacity to love unconditionally and with good intentions.

MARCH 29

"Every relationship, good or bad, is a mirror, reflecting back to us who we are, what we need, how we love, and what we should avoid."

Every relationship we form acts as a mirror, allowing us to gain insights into what we need and how we'd like to be loved, even the ways in which we care for others. It is also a window into the things that don't serve our well-being. When a relationship is healthy, we learn about our capacity for love, compromise, and understanding. Unhealthy ones reveal our unmet needs, areas in which we need to nurture for growth, and the boundaries we need to establish with the people we allow into our lives. Every relationship, whether joyful or overrun with pain, ultimately contributes to our self-awareness and acts as a guide toward a more present and fulfilling way of interacting with the world and the people in it.

MARCH 30

"Walking away is tough, but the most painful goodbyes are the ones that help us grow."

S evering ties with someone you dreamed of forever with can be emotionally taxing; it's often through these most painful goodbyes that we gain the most significant opportunities for personal growth and self-improvement.

MARCH 31

"Being single is better than being in a
relationship in which you feel alone."

C hoosing to be single over being in a relationship in which you
feel lonely shows that you put your mental health and self-
respect first.

APRIL 1

"Accepting that it's over is the
beginning of a path toward healing."

Acknowledging the end of something—be it a relationship, a phase of life, a job, a friendship, or a cherished dream—marks the starting point of a healing journey. Acknowledging the end paves the way for emotional freedom, allowing us to confront our pain and grief instead of suppressing everything we don't actually want to feel, which is an important step in the process of healing.

APRIL 2

"The pain in your heart is not a weakness; it's a testament to your capacity to be truthful about the way you love."

E xperiencing heartache is not indicative of weakness; rather, it's a powerful testament to your honesty and the true depth of your emotions. It shows that you have loved deeply, even when the outcome was not as you had desired.

April 3

"Moving on doesn't mean forgetting;
it means deciding to cultivate
peace after a chaotic and unhealthy
relationship."

The process of moving on isn't about erasing past experiences; instead, it implies making a clear and conscious decision to seek out peace even in the midst of chaos.

APRIL 4

"Sometimes, the value of a relationship is not in it lasting but in the lessons it teaches when it ends."

Sometimes, the true worth of a relationship lies not in its longevity but in the valuable insights we gain when it's all said and done. When relationships end, they often expose our strengths and weaknesses. The ending of a relationship reveals the truth that we desire and presents opportunities for self-improvement and understanding.

APRIL 5

"You have to accept that sometimes the person you want to create a future with is best left behind in the past."

There will be times when the person you choose will not be able to fit into the future you've dreamed up in your head. And though this may cause you a great deal of pain, in time, you realize the losses provide space for something beautiful to be gained.

APRIL 6

"Loss is a profound moment on the
journey to gaining something better."

Though loss can be one of the most painful and difficult feelings
to navigate, it often serves as a significant turning point on the
path to gaining something more fitting to your needs. It forces us to
confront the truth of what we're feeling and the incoming changes
that we sometimes fear, and it lends us lessons on how to adapt. This
fosters personal growth and resilience.

APRIL 7

"It's easy to see a broken heart has
some sort of weakness, but a heart
that has been broken has shown
that it is strong enough to love
unconditionally."

A broken heart is often mistakenly perceived as a moment of weakness when, in fact, it is a testament to the profound capacity to feel and genuinely love something outside of yourself. It's a resilience born from the courage to open yourself fully to another, even in the face of potential heartache and sorrow.

April 8

"Sometimes, you have to lose a person to find more of yourself."

E very so often, the departure of a person from your life can prompt a journey of self-reflection, enabling you to discover and embrace more aspects of who you truly are. In this process, you discover just how easily loss can lead to gain. Through this realization, you begin to foster a deeper understanding of your needs.

April 9

"Needing closure is not a reason to compromise your progress toward walking away for good."

While seeking closure is a natural part of healing, it should not compromise your progress toward severing ties that no longer serve your heart. The desire for closure can also be used as manipulation by the person you're attempting to leave behind. Prioritizing your healing is important, even if it means foregoing traditional notions of closure for the sake of moving forward on your own terms.

APRIL 10

"The moment you realize your true
worth is the moment you decide that
you are no longer willing to settle for
less than you deserve."

Recognizing the true value of your presence and placing greater importance on the decision to no longer accept anything that falls short of your worth: this newfound self-awareness and respect can effectively elevate your standards and will always ensure that your choice of a partner aligns with your deserved level of treatment and happiness.

APRIL 11

"You can never fully heal, returning to someone incapable of loving you the way you needed."

When you return to someone who fails to love you in the manner you need, you hinder your healing process, preventing you from reaching a state of complete emotional recovery. True healing will often require you to distance yourself from the source of pain.

APRIL 12

"You might believe that letting go
means giving up, but in fact, moving
on is not quitting; it's realizing that
you deserve better."

While it might be tempting to see the act of letting go
as surrendering, in truth, moving on signifies a bold
acknowledgment of your self-worth and the comprehension that you
deserve more.

APRIL 13

"Each heartbreak is a stepping-stone toward the love you deserve."

E ach instance of heartbreak, while painful, serves as a stepping-stone on your journey toward a life filled with things that cherish your presence. They are lessons that shape your understanding of what you deserve and what to avoid.

APRIL 14

"Today it's painful, but tomorrow it's strength."

The pain you endure today, while challenging, becomes the bedrock of your resilience and strength for the future. Each struggle is an opportunity for growth, a chance for transformation. This is you evolved into more than previously believed capable.

APRIL 15

"Your self-worth can't be defined by
those who do not see it."

The value of your heart is not determined by the perception of those who fail to recognize it. Your self-worth is defined by your own understanding and self-affirmation.

APRIL 16

"There are nights when a breakup is a nightmare, and there are some nights when it feels like the best dream."

E ven in heartache's darkest nights, remember that pain paves the path to freedom that is often the hardest to reach because most people would rather look away than stare into the truth of the pain they feel. The sweetest dreams often follow the toughest wake-up calls. In facing your darkest moments, you can transform a nightmare into paradise.

APRIL 17

"Love becomes sadness when it's taken for granted, and the pain you feel right now is love without a home or place to go."

I n those moments of sadness, on those days when you feel depressed, and on those nights when you struggle to get sleep, trust that there is an opportunity for your focus, time, and energy to be turned inward. Trust that the loneliness you feel is an opportunity to love yourself.

APRIL 18

"Never apologize for crying over
something that once made you
believe in a future filled with love."

I n the turbulence of sorrow, remember your emotions are waves,
not an ocean, especially those troubling feelings in your chest.
Anchor yourself in self-love, prioritizing your deservingness over
temporary storms of sadness.

April 19

"It hurts deeply because you love deeply. The pain is a testament to your courage to feel."

Be patient with your healing process; it's okay to have days that are harder than others. Self-love is a journey, not a destination. Take this time to reconnect with yourself, to explore your own desires, dreams, and passions. Remember that you are enough, just as you are, and that the love you give to yourself is the most powerful love of all.

APRIL 20

"A bitter end can become a
beautiful start."

I want you to understand the power of your never-ending love, the way your heart continues to beat, even in the absence of the person you thought you'd build a lasting relationship with. I want you to remember just how often you've been in this place and how often you were capable of making it to the other side. Repeat after me: "The ending is the beginning."

APRIL 21

"In the midst of a breakup, it's important to focus on what you deserve and not entirely on how you feel."

There is often a difference in how you feel and what you deserve. The goal is to eventually get to a place where what you feel creates a process that leads you in the direction of what you deserve. Sometimes, you care about a person who isn't aligned with the version of life and love that you need, and so, though this road is rough, you learn so much about yourself from loving the wrong person. You may feel loss, you may feel as though loving them will be enough, but none of what you have in your heart will be valued by a person who is wrong for you.

APRIL 22

"There's a thought of what you want, there's belief in what you deserve, but having your heart broken teaches you what you need."

Unhealthy relationships are laced with wisdom. The relationships that aren't meant to last will usually teach you how to cultivate the ones that do.

April 23

"You destroy your chances of taking flight when you refuse to let go of what weighs you down."

The wrong relationships force you to carry around a weight that destroys your chance to soar, grow, and transform. Think back to what that person makes you feel, and understand that you can only rise in a relationship that doesn't require you to compromise your peace.

April 24

"When a relationship ends, you're
not losing yourself. You only lose a
version of a future that isn't aligned
with the version of life you deserve."

Endings can be tough, but they are also opportunities for self-discovery. As you navigate the waters of a breakup, remember to treat yourself with kindness and patience. Allow yourself time to grieve, to heal, and to grow. Self-love isn't just about feeling good—it's about setting healthy boundaries, saying no when you need to, choosing yourself even when others overlook you, and saying yes to what makes you truly happy.

APRIL 25

"Sometimes, you look back on a past
relationship not because you want to
go back but because you need more
inspiration to move forward."

Reflecting on the past isn't always a longing for what you left behind; often, it's the fuel propelling your journey forward. Each memory serves as proof that you are deserving of so much more.

APRIL 26

"Be honest with yourself. Cry and
forgive. Learn. Move on. Let your tears
create a river so that what no longer
belongs to you can flow out of your
life. Let your tears become the water
that nurtures the seeds of your future."

Tears cleanse the soul, paving the way for forgiveness and growth;
they're the river washing away what no longer serves you.
Embrace this action; this expression is vital, for it waters the seeds of
your future, promoting a lush garden of resilience and providing a
map to new beginnings.

APRIL 27

"You're struggling to leave a person
who has already abandoned you."

Embrace the courage to walk away from what has left you. Move closer to the love that has always resided in your heart. You will find in your moment of loss that you alone are capable of filling yourself even when you're running on empty.

APRIL 28

"When you stop focusing on what a
relationship could've been, you're
free to see what that relationship
actually was."

D on't let the what-ifs plague reality with a foggy fantasy of
what could have been. When you focus on the potential of a
person rather than their actual actions, you almost trick yourself into
believing that things can be better than they've been when, in truth,
nothing will change.

APRIL 29

"Sometimes, you just have to let go
of certain people in order to make
room for something beautiful to enter
your life."

L etting go is the key to opening new doors. The reward in moving
on is the joy of new connections, strong connections, and the
opportunity to discover what it means to be with someone who is
willing to match your effort.

APRIL 30

"Hard to believe in a love that feels
like joy when you've settled for a love
that resembles hell."

It's hard to notice the flower's bloom when you're fixated on the dead roses wilting in the corner, in a vase, given to you by someone who never lived up to the love they promised.

MAY 1

"Your softness is not a weakness; your kindness is your strength."

Embrace the softness in your soul and the kindness that dwells in your heart; they're not points of weakness but powerful sources of strength.

MAY 2

"Stop making the wrong people feel
special. No matter how hard you try,
they'll never be right for you."

S top spending valuable energy on those who can't honor your
worth. True connection is not forced but is mutually devoted.

MAY 3

"The heartbreak you feel will inspire
you to grow. The need for something
better will fuel the journey after
the breakup."

Never underestimate your strength, and don't let a breakup define your self-worth. You are more than a relationship; you are a person of kindness, devotion, and truth. Within your heart lies an infinite potential for genuine love. Honor your journey, and respect your own timing. This is your life; run it at your own pace.

MAY 4

"Moving on is the act of turning your love inward."

The choice to walk away is often an expression of self-love. The moment you decide to move forward with your life, you give yourself the time and space needed to begin the process of healing. You don't always have to leave a person because you hate them; sometimes, you leave someone because your love for self is greater.

MAY 5

"You may not realize it now, but saying
goodbye in this moment means
saying hello to something better later."

Y ou've been here before; it's just easy to forget the several
moments when your strength and courage were on full display.
You unknowingly find new and beautiful ways to create a path that
leads you to something better than what you've had.

MAY 6

"The more you love yourself, the
more you make room for healing in
your heart."

I like to think of self-love as protection, a shield of some sort. I believe that the more you practice self-love, the less likely you are to fall victim to those who have bad intentions. In the event of the ending of a relationship, I believe self-love to be vital, for it forces distance between yourself and the things that hurt you. The more distance between you and things that no longer serve your idea of peace, the more space you are provided to practice healing.

MAY 7

"The closure isn't in the goodbye, nor does it remain with the person who hurt you. Closure is what happens when you rediscover yourself after heartbreak."

We have to change the way we see closure, its definition, and the truth in what it actually means. I think it's natural to wonder why something ended or why that person decided to hurt you, but the truth is, sometimes people do bad things because it's tolerated, and sometimes the person you believed to be "the one" had always intended to let you down. The idea of closure can often serve as an emotional prison, leaving one in limbo and causing oneself to remain stuck, asking questions that will never be answered. It's time to look inward for the truth. It's time to retrospect on all that has happened and come up with your own understanding of what transpired. True closure is what happens when you realize you are better off alone.

MAY 8

"Healing is a road that leads you back
into your own arms."

I t's important to understand the dangers of outsourcing your
healing to external things and or other people. The use of
someone else to make things feel better is a cycle that leads you to the
type of relationships you need to heal from in the first place. For one,
there are people who prey upon those who feel empty or broken at
the end of a relationship. And the idea of looking within yourself as a
resource of healing doesn't mean you have to do it alone. It just means
you need to act in the best interest of the health of mind and heart.

MAY 9

"In this melody of life, the pain is just a pause, not a stop, not the end."

The pain you feel right now is temporary; it's the thing that is felt before the breakthrough. A setback is just a reset. Don't give up on yourself.

MAY 10

"One-sided love is a melody being
played on a piano with a single key."

The composition of a beautiful future can't be expressed by two people who are out of tune with one another. Genuine love is a two-sided affair; don't settle.

May 11

"Never leave yourself again for someone who can't love you in the way you need."

I t's tempting to go back, especially when the person who hurts you begins to speak the language that you were speaking the entire time. They make promises to do everything you expect of them; they use the hope that remains in your heart against you just so that they can have another opportunity at something they don't deserve. Don't leave yourself for someone who left you a long time ago.

MAY 12

"The breakup may hurt your heart,

but the moment you begin to focus

on yourself, you find that there

had always been a treasure hidden

beneath the heartache."

You are the gift; you are the prize. The reward for letting go is you.

MAY 13

"Your best companion is the person you see standing alone in the mirror."

The reflection you see in the mirror is more than just an image of yourself; it's your most faithful ally and friend through life's journey and the several ups and downs of being in love. Nurture this companionship, for it fosters strength and the courage to take the best path that serves you.

MAY 14

"The end of a relationship is the
beginning of a cocoon. Self-love
reveals the butterfly."

Post-breakup is a journey of metamorphosis, a profound
instance of transformation; the cocoon of heartache yields
self-reflection and emotional growth. As the old relationship fades,
new understandings emerge. This transformation, though painful,
lays the foundation for healthy relationships with others and a deeper
connection to self.

MAY 15

"A flower doesn't need a companion to bloom."

I was walking near Central Park one day in New York City, and I happened to spot a lonesome flower blooming on its own. I immediately thought about my loved ones who had experienced heartbreak and even those of you who may be reading this now. Even in your loneliest of hours, you can still be everything you're meant to be. When you understand this, you will no longer willingly give up your peace of mind just to be with someone who will let you down.

MAY 16

"A breakup is not the edge of a cliff;
it's ground beside a new mountain
to climb."

I n truth, in every end, you find something or someone else to love, but maybe this time, you are the adventure. Maybe this time, you are that someone new.

MAY 17

"Sometimes, a relationship ends
because your life is meant to travel in
a more beautiful direction."

A detour is necessary because there's a better route to take.
Nothing is set in stone, no matter how much you love someone.
Sometimes, relationships end because someone else is better
equipped to love you.

MAY 18

"The brokenness you feel is
uncomfortable, but the cracks allow
for light to enter."

There is always a silver lining to all the painful experiences in this life. It's not easy to see the blessing in your anguish, but that transition between where you've been and where you're going is a chance to choose what direction to take. Choose wisely.

MAY 19

"Your value and self-worth are not measured by the pain of every heartbreak you've experienced."

The end of a relationship may change your circumstances, but it doesn't alter the essence of who you are or diminish the value you bring into a relationship. Remember, you are not defined by an ended relationship but by the strength you display when it's over.

MAY 20

"Breakups are only a comma in your story of finding genuine love."

You'll flip through a few pages, even linger on some, until you find a story worthy of the rest of your life. I don't know where exactly you are in your book, but I hope that you're only a couple of pages away from reading something beautiful.

MAY 21

"If you listen closely to the silence that follows a breakup, you can hear a song of self-love beginning to fade in."

Though many years ago, I can still recall those restless nights when the silence was deafening; it is then when I uncovered a new melody worth listening to, and the sounds of self-love, when followed, showed me a way out from the suffering.

MAY 22

"Sometimes, the heart needs to break

so that it can beat stronger."

T he lessons you learn in the midst of heartbreak can be utilized as a stronger foundation for your heart to be built upon.

MAY 23

"The end of a relationship is a detour, not a dead end."

The breakup is not a dead end but a detour that guides you toward a route that best serves you and fulfills your need for genuine love. Embrace these redirections, and be patient on this journey.

MAY 24

"Sometimes, you lose people to make the journey back to yourself less difficult."

Some people are just distractions; they keep you from the healthy practices that would otherwise encourage you to leave them behind. You've been trying to find yourself, and, in doing so, you will lose anyone who stands in your way.

MAY 25

"Letting go is a version of love that doesn't involve possessing or keeping a person who no longer fits into the plans of your life."

Letting go not only saves you but also helps the other person be with someone who fits into their plans. I like to think that sometimes "I love you" means "I'm setting you free."

MAY 26

"The breakup is a seed, the future
is the flower, and self-love is what
makes it grow."

F unny how there is life waiting in the death of a relationship that wasn't meant to last. The breakup itself becomes a seed that, when nourished with the lessons you've learned, begins to sprout out a future in which you can fully bloom.

MAY 27

"You don't have to be perfect to deserve unconditional love."

Perfection is not a prerequisite for deserving real love. You are worthy, despite being overlooked or unappreciated. Unconditional love cherishes you in its entirety. Preserve your heart for someone who understands that.

MAY 28

"From the ashes of sorrow, a phoenix
forged from the fire of loss is born."

Amid the ashes of heartbreak, a phoenix finds life forged by
the intense flames of loss. This symbol of your resilience is a
testament to your capacity to endure hardship, transforming pain
into power. You are much stronger than you feel, and today, you are
closer to a life that is aligned with what your heart needs.

MAY 29

"Embrace yourself; you are a never-ending love story. A love that never leaves."

E mbracing self-love means recognizing your own worth and taking care of your needs. Be gentle with yourself in your time of need, just as you would with a close friend enduring some of the same things you're experiencing right now. Your emotions are valid, and it's okay to give yourself the time and space you need to heal. You are deserving of your own understanding and patience.

MAY 30

"The breakup is a wake-up call often mistaken as a breakdown."

A breakup, often mistaken as a personal breakdown, is actually a powerful wake-up call, pushing toward self-reflection and growth. It ignites a spotlight that becomes focused on your relationship patterns, your needs, and your worth.

MAY 31

"Every tear shed over lost love
waters the roots of a flower's most
beautiful future."

E very tear shed over a lost love is not just a sign of sadness but also a nurturing drop that feeds the roots of your future and the love that awaits you. Just as water feeds a flower, your tears of heartache nourish the evolution of your mind, heart, and soul.

JUNE 1

"The heartbreak you've been feeling is
not a roadblock but a speed bump on
love's highway."

L isten, I know it's painful, and, right now, you may feel stuck in
the aftermath of something you thought would last. It's okay to
feel this way; it's okay to grieve the loss of love. But remember, your
current state of mind is not your final destination.

JUNE 2

"Even if it doesn't feel like it at the moment, you are the lighthouse guiding your broken heart through the storm of a breakup. Self-love will help you find your way to shore."

I need you to understand something. It's natural to feel lost when a relationship is over. In these moments, it may be challenging to see that you are, in fact, the lighthouse guiding your own heart through the storm because, right now, the wounds are fresh, and you are too close to the pain. But just as a lighthouse stands with an unwavering power amid turbulent waves, so too does the core essence of who you are.

June 3

"The aftermath of heartbreak is a scene filled with wisdom, strength, and self-growth."

In the wake of heartbreak, the landscape might seem desolate, painted using hues of loss and sadness. Yet, if you look closer, it's also rich with wisdom and a chance to grow beyond what you thought capable.

JUNE 4

"Love yourself so deeply that you
refuse to allow them back into
your heart."

S elf-love is a powerful fortress, a safeguard for your heart against everything that once wounded it. When you love yourself profoundly, it's not just about cherishing your strengths and achievements; it's also about protecting yourself from anyone who wants to stand between you and your heart's desire for peace.

JUNE 5

"Being single is an opportunity to
rebuild a stronger, wiser self."

There's nothing wrong with deciding to be alone, especially
when it means the absence of being in a relationship that alters
your peace and dictates your emotional experiences in a negative way.
Being single is an opportunity to rebuild what was broken and repair
the things that require your attention. Take your time, and focus on
yourself. Pay attention to what you need and understand so that you
can provide everything you want.

JUNE 6

"Being single serves as an offering of
your love unto yourself."

W hen you go searching for someone to love, never overlook
yourself. Remember that you are just as deserving of the love
you've given to others.

JUNE 7

"Your heart is not a bargaining chip."

Using your heart as a bargaining chip will always mean compromising your emotional well-being for something you want but possibly don't need, which can lead to emotional trauma. It could also result in being in a relationship in which you're always giving more than you receive, which will lead to feelings of resentment and dissatisfaction.

JUNE 8

"In the ruins of heartbreak, written on every piece of a broken heart is a story that provides a foundation for new beginnings."

It's beautiful the way you've encountered so much pain and yet you stand strong in your belief that you deserve more than what you've had in the past. You're writing the pages of your love story, and sometimes those pages get tainted with passages of lies, betrayal, and unbearable emotions, but in the end, you pick up your pen and decide to keep writing.

JUNE 9

"You find the courage to move on
by understanding that where
you're headed is better than where
you've been."

The past is not a place to live your life, and the things that live there are no longer worthy of a space in your present. Understand that where you're headed is far more beautiful than where you've been and that sometimes the things you wanted have to be left behind because none of those things are what you need.

JUNE 10

"Cherish being single. It is there
in solitude that you discover the
strength and courage to fall in love
with yourself."

You are a complete individual, capable of independently fostering joy, peace, love, and fulfillment. Remember, a relationship is not the sole measure of your happiness or success. Use the periods that often feel like a breakdown to cultivate self-love in order to discover passions and pursuits that truly make your soul sing. There is immense power in learning to enjoy your own company.

June 11

"Most of the time, being single is
not about loneliness; it's about
discovering how complete you feel
even when you're by yourself."

Peace magnifies your strength. Peace is a space that allows clarity and self-realization. When a relationship is over, you are granted greater moments of solitude; it is then when you will discover your voice and the courage to speak against everything you don't want, and it is then when you will learn to speak the right things into your life.

JUNE 12

"The most valuable currency in a breakup is trust. You have to trust that when someone betrays you, that just means there's something better out there for you."

You will never be able to keep what isn't meant to be kept. And the truth you seek will never be found in someone who is content with lying to you. Trust is vital: trust in yourself and your belief in what you deserve. You have to trust your natural reaction to the way they make you feel. You have to trust that, when someone loves you, they won't put themselves in a position to lose you.

June 13

"Don't rush back out of fear and loneliness into the arms of the person who hurt you. Patience will bring you something beautiful."

The allure of familiar territory, despite the pain that lives there, can often be overwhelming, especially when faced with feelings of loneliness. However, it's important to remember that past actions often serve as a guide to future behavior, and rushing back into the arms of someone who has caused you pain can potentially set you up for recurring heartache.

JUNE 14

"Let go of what is wrong for you
so that you can grow closer to
something right."

C linging to an unhealthy relationship often stems from a place of fear and complacency. When your hands are focused on holding on to the wrong things, you miss the opportunity to reach for what your heart deserves.

JUNE 15

"The relationship you cultivate with yourself sets the tone for all other relationships."

The relationship we foster with ourselves creates the foundation of our interactions with others. Our perception of ourselves influences how we allow others to treat us and the boundaries we set. If we are kind to ourselves, respectful, and understanding, we not only cultivate a healthy sense of self-worth but we also set the standard for how we expect to be treated by others.

Conversely, a negative self-relationship can lead to harmful patterns, as we might unintentionally attract and accept the wrong treatment from the people we care about.

JUNE 16

"Being single is a chance to create a
profoundly intimate relationship
with yourself."

It's important to remember that solitude, while sometimes intimidating, isn't synonymous with loneliness. It can be a period of introspection, growth, and self-discovery.

JUNE 17

"Good or bad, each relationship
teaches us something. Appreciate the
lesson, but don't let it be a distraction."

E very relationship we encounter, whether gratifying or overrun
with challenges, is a vessel for learning. The pain you feel is a
key that unlocks the door to tranquility. Experiencing chaos makes it
easier to recognize the pathway to peace of mind.

JUNE 18

"Be with someone who doesn't
suppress your spirit; you deserve to
be elevated and appreciated for who
you truly are."

Have you ever been in a relationship that required you to shrink yourself just to make the other person feel comfortable with who you are? These types of relationships cause you to compromise everything that makes you feel fulfilled and happy. You do this out of care without understanding that if that person felt the same way you do, they wouldn't require you to be less than you are. Be with someone who is comfortable with your best self.

JUNE 19

"Remember this: In order to cultivate
and maintain a healthy relationship,
you are required to be healthy first."

A tree must first be healthy at the root to yield fruit; so must an individual be healthy—mentally, emotionally, and physically—to contribute to a relationship that thrives.

JUNE 20

"Before you expect to be understood,
be sure that you understand
yourself first."

Before we can accurately communicate our feelings, thoughts, or desires to others, we first need to comprehend them for ourselves. This type of understanding is an ongoing process of introspection, one that helps us recognize our values, emotional triggers, strengths, weaknesses, and aspirations.

June 21

"Being single is not about waiting around for life to start; it's about living the fullness of your life on your own."

Being single is not a waiting area; it's a space where you can freely focus all of your energy on yourself and cultivate a life that is absent of all the things and all the people who do not deserve to take up residence in your life. When you are single, you receive a profound and vital opportunity to truly understand who you are and or who you'd like to be moving forward.

JUNE 22

"A good relationship doesn't have to be perfect, and you don't have to be perfect to deserve a good relationship."

A successful relationship doesn't require you to remain flawless. Your imperfections should not prohibit you from having a healthy, fulfilling partnership. In truth, it's about accepting and navigating through imperfections both in ourselves and our relationships. It's about the will to learn from our mistakes, apply those lessons, and attempt to do better by one another.

JUNE 23

"That initial realization of the peace you experience in being single can be empowering; embrace it."

Take a moment to look around. Be present where you are, cling to that bit of silence, the solitude. In the absence of everything you thought you needed, you are complete, you are at peace, and you are safe. Embrace this moment, and extend it for as long as you can.

JUNE 24

"Being single is about growth, so much so that when you enter the right relationship, you will blossom in new and beautiful ways."

Embrace the single life; it is here where you will develop the ability to be all that you can be for yourself, which will make it easier to not only be everything with someone else but also be able to spot those who are willing to match your effort.

JUNE 25

"The person who truly loves you will admire your solitude, not fear it."

The right relationship offers you an opportunity to be with someone who will not only remain by your side but also give you space to be all that you are whenever you need it.

JUNE 26

"When you're single, you stand on your own, looking into a mirror, and you reflect true love and devotion. You have everything you need, even in the loss of a relationship."

Remember this always, especially in your loneliest moments. You may think that being alone means you're missing something, but in being on your own, you have everything you need. Your single self is more than enough, and you are capable of providing more for yourself than what your previous relationship could.

JUNE 27

"Do not live with the past. Move on, because everything worthy of your energy is waiting in the distance, beyond the relationships that didn't work."

You can't live your life moving backward. Focusing your energy on what's behind you threatens the future you deserve. I know you can move on because you've displayed the courage to face the truth in what you feel; that's why your eyes are moving left to right, consuming these words. It's not an easy task; moving forward takes time and discipline. But remember that what's up ahead is a representation of everything that the people you've left behind distracted you from. And, in order to live out your dreams, you have to stop focusing on what caused the nightmare.

JUNE 28

"The right relationship will not cause you to compromise your individuality."

Healthy relationships are built and maintained by people who know who they are on their own, and with that clarity and understanding, they come together to form something beautiful. You should feel encouraged by your partner in your efforts to care for yourself and to fully explore all that you are without feeling as if you need to make yourself feel small. Someone who genuinely loves you will not require you to dim your light so that they can shine.

June 29

"Being single is a celebration of the fact that you are capable of giving yourself all the things that people refuse to give you."

When you are single, you are free to focus solely on what you need without fear of being labeled selfish. Oftentimes, self-care can be mistaken for selfishness, but understand that you can only do for others when you've done for yourself. Take a moment to cultivate and maintain whatever it is you need in order to heal and prepare yourself to fully adapt to what it means to be on your own.

JUNE 30

"Don't fear the path of the single life;
embrace the silence, the freedom, the
peace, and the possibilities."

There was a silence soon after, a silence that I'd never known before, a silence that I didn't even know I needed, but when that relationship was over, despite the pain I felt, there was freedom sprinkled in every corner. Places where sadness had always lived. Ultimately, there's this level of peace, a heavy one that follows the absence of people who don't deserve to be in your life, and sometimes that peace is mistaken for something negative. Still, it's beautiful when you begin to embrace the idea that you're better off alone than with someone who hurts your heart. Embrace that feeling, and protect it.

July 1

"The right relationship will never distract you from experiencing the things you need to feel in order to be your best."

A healthy relationship will not hinder the practice of self-care but rather support and enhance it. Your emotional well-being should not be compromised in an effort to benefit the relationship when, in truth, it is vital to the success of one. The right relationship aids your journey toward your best emotional state rather than detracting from it.

JULY 2

"The journey of being single can lead you to many destinations. Cherish the roads you take alone."

Being single is a journey, a solo road trip through life's expansive landscapes. Each experience, choice, and moment of self-discovery is like a new city you pass through, each with its own unique lessons. During this journey, you're the driver, with full control of the wheel, deciding when to accelerate, when to pause, and which routes to take. This gives you the opportunity to explore who you truly are. This journey will be a beautiful one, even with its highs and lows.

July 3

"Whether single or in a relationship, remember, you are worthy of a love you never have to question."

The belief that you deserve someone faithful should always reside somewhere in your heart. It's easy to forget what you deserve when you've decided to settle out of fear of being alone. A relationship filled with questions will never be able to give you the answers you need. When you're busy wondering what will happen, or constantly finding yourself in limbo, you miss out on what it means to live in love.

JULY 4

"When you're with the right person,
you are closer to creating the right
relationship. It's that simple."

T hink for a second about what makes your heart smile; now ask yourself whether this is a distant idea or whether it is in reach. When you're with the right person, what you need outside of yourself is in arm's reach, but if the joy you require and the peace you seek is somewhere lost in the distance, then consider moving on. The right person is not a perfect person, but they're also not someone who tries to imprison you in a place of sadness and regret.

July 5

"The single life is an opportunity to shine without a shadow or shade. Celebrate these moments."

Being single is an opportunity to prioritize yourself. Being single is a chance to focus solely on yourself without dealing with whispers or criticism of being selfish. There is nothing wrong with turning your interests inward. You are not wrong for focusing all of your energy into healing and growth.

July 6

"Being single means that you have the courage needed to preserve your time and energy for someone who deserves it."

It's beautiful, deciding to be on your own and refusing to chase others in search of a readily available peace that's within you once you decide to look inward. It is a brave thing to choose to be alone when your natural reaction to it is to look for someone's company to be in. This is a reminder that you can have everything when "you" is all there is.

JULY 7

"Don't rush; avoid hurry. Do all things quietly with a calm spirit, including the love you are giving."

Don't be in a rush to find someone new. Usually after a breakup, you are more likely to run into slightly different versions of the person you're trying to get over. It is only after you practice healing and self-love that you broaden your horizons, increasing your chances of attracting the proper mate.

JULY 8

"Though heartbreak may cast a dark shadow, remember that every sunset is a promise of a beautiful sunrise."

The pain you feel right now is not the end. The heartbreak you feel right now is an emotional bridge that can and will lead you to wellness. Though your restless nights may bleed into the mornings, each day is an opportunity to be stronger; each day is an opportunity to access the lessons given unto you from a love that has been lost.

July 9

"Relationships are like mirrors in the way that sometimes they break, and it's better to leave the pieces where they are than to hurt yourself trying to put them back together."

Attempting to fix something that is meant to stay broken is a cycle some of us know all too well. The more you try, the worse it gets. And even when you think you've made progress, what now sits in front of you is something you hardly recognize. Just like the trust that is broken, there are things that can be done to a relationship that deem it impossible to put back together, and while this realization hurts, it's also important to see the shattered pieces as a symbol of what you were capable of cultivating in the first place. What I mean by this is that the most profound damage often comes from the greatest capacity to love someone outside of yourself. So, while at first you see what is broken, you can also see what you were willing to create.

JULY 10

"The heartache from your past is a lighthouse guiding you away from the waves of similar mistakes."

Sometimes, it's the memory of what was that helps you discover what could be. Your mistakes create a map that can help you travel more seamlessly on this journey.

JULY 11

"Do not let the tears of your past drown you; instead, let them nourish the beauty and growth of the days that lie ahead."

Think of your past moments, even the difficult ones that brought you tears, as rain showers. Yes, at times, they may have been heavy and uncomfortable, but they also serve a crucial role in your personal development and growth. These showers, filled with lessons of wisdom and courage, don't exist to drown you in sorrow but to nourish the soil of your present so that your future can bloom beautifully.

JULY 12

"Sometimes, you have to burn bridges

so that something stronger can rise

from the ashes."

You thought burning that bridge would keep you stuck. What you didn't realize was that, come winter, the warmth would help you survive and that, in place of that gap between you and the journey ahead, you would go on to build something stronger: a bridge in a different direction, a new and beautiful path to take.

JULY 13

"When one door of potential love closes, the window to self-love and healing opens."

Right now, more than anything or anyone else, you deserve you. Sometimes, the door leading you elsewhere closes so that you can turn your focus to the window opening up to yourself.

JULY 14

"Today's darkness is tomorrow's light."

While it may be bleak and dark, today always has something to be learned from in the moments when you feel like the lessons are not visible. If you can manage some sort of clarity, you'll figure out that life's problems often lead to solutions; just as the night becomes day, the terrible feeling can be transformed into delight.

JULY 15

"Heartbreak is tough, but, like the raging sea, it guides you toward the shores of wisdom and resilience."

You are everything, despite being treated as if you have nothing to offer. You are valuable even when others are blind to your worth. You are brilliant even in the aftermath of choosing the wrong person. And you are strong, despite feeling broken.

July 16

"In the garden that is your heart,
let this pain be the compost that
nourishes your soul and helps your
heart bloom again."

Your heart truly is a garden, and any emotional pain you experience is a sort of compost. While compost might not be the most pleasant thing, it's a powerful fertilizer that transforms dead soil into a fertile oasis that promotes vibrant and healthy growth. Similarly, the pain you're experiencing right now, although uncomfortable and sometimes depressing, can act as a rich compost for your heart. It introduces essential nutrients of courage and compassion into your life's soil.

JULY 17

"Every tear is a lesson dropped
into the lake of wisdom and
self-realization."

Visualize every tear you shed as a droplet falling into a lake of wisdom and peace. This lake represents a greater understanding of self. Each tear, regardless of its origin, carries a valuable lesson about life and relationships.

JULY 18

"The ending of one plot is the beginning of a new story. Keep going; you're not finished yet."

We look upon each ending with fear because we're blinded by our emotional pain, so much so that we do not realize the blessing waiting on the other side. The ending is only part of the story; the next chapter is a new beginning.

JULY 19

"The silence after a breakup is a moment of introspection, a time for meditation and healing."

The relationships that don't work can serve as steps on the stairway to the life and love you've been longing for. As you continue the process of building this stairway, don't forget to take frequent breaks to practice self-love.

July 20

"It's easy to forget how strong you are
when a relationship ends, but your
heart has always been an ocean that
can survive the chaos of any storm."

You are stronger than you've given yourself credit for. Many times, your resilience has been on display. Whether it was a friendship or a romantic relationship, you have always proven that you can transform an ending into a fresh start.

JULY 21

"The shattered glass of a broken heart will eventually reflect the light of love, healing, and wisdom with each fragment."

I magine heartbreak as glass shattering into many pieces. It's easy to feel consumed by the jagged edges and scattered fragments, each one a painful reminder of what once was. However, think of these fragments as tiny mirrors, each piece capable of reflecting light that will help guide you somewhere safe.

JULY 22

"Every teardrop will water the seeds of
your future love."

Y ou face the destruction of your heart so that you know what to
fix and where to begin. You cry so that you can replenish your
soul. Every drop is a form of renewal and transformation.

JULY 23

"Breakups sculpt the heart into
structures of resilience and courage."

Y ou are the sculptor; the breakup will be the tools you use to forge something beautiful. Initially, this process might be painful and hard to endure, as old habits and or attachments, similar to marble, are chipped away over time. But, just as a sculptor has the ability to carve a beautiful statue from a rough material, breakups, in their own way, shape your heart into a form of strength and courage.

July 24

"Heartbreak is a winter, a season to be still, a resting place for the seeds of something beautiful waiting to bloom."

I believe that heartbreak is best compared to a harsh winter, the coldest and seemingly barren season. It might seem as if all life has retreated, leaving behind a desolate place. However, beneath the surface of what the eyes witness is a critical event taking place. Winter is a period of rest, where seeds lie dormant in waiting to grow. Similarly, heartbreak can often be viewed as a necessary phase of stillness, a resting place, a soil for your emotional seeds. During this season, there is an opportunity to reflect on how best to nurture these seeds for optimum growth. While the process might seem uncomfortable and lonely, remember that this is merely a phase, not a permanent state.

July 25

"Lost love is a falling leaf, allowing

new growth for a new season of love."

A falling leaf is just an end of a phase before more life grows in its place. The phase of your unhappiness will end and give way to something new and exciting. Be still; be patient with yourself.

JULY 26

"It's scary in the beginning; it hurts in ways you never imagined. But your heartbreak is like the moon; the darker the night, the brighter its glow."

Initially, heartbreak may come off as an all-encompassing darkness, similar to when the night first sets in. The darkness is a representation of the pain and the sorrow you feel, which is often overwhelming and appears to be never-ending. However, just as the moon finds a way to rise and shine its brightest when the night sky is its darkest, your heart remains luminous, able to light the restless journey through the night.

July 27

"If you listen closely, you can hear the whispers of self-love in the echoes of sadness."

In a moment's notice, everything you've been working toward can end abruptly, and you immediately go into a panic about what your future will be, but it's important to breathe and focus on this moment, this day. Face the things that hurt you so that you can heal yourself.

July 28

"Sometimes, you have to walk away from the person you thought you needed so that you can see that the only arms worth holding you are your own."

S elf-love is vital because it helps you create an otherwise nonexistent road that will lead you to things that will not threaten the health of your heart.

JULY 29

"A night of heartbreak bleeds into a dawn of self-love."

The darkest part of every night is usually followed by the warm and enchanting light of the sun taking its rightful place in the sky. It's a lonely journey, but you will find a way to see the sun.

JULY 30

"Letting go is a beautiful act of self-love."

When you decide to let go, you are simply reminding yourself that nothing is more important than your peace of mind and health of heart. Choose yourself today, especially in the face of those who have chosen to neglect you.

JULY 31

"Being single is an opportunity, not a punishment."

There is freedom in the aftermath of a breakup. It's just hard to embrace it because you never intended to let go in the first place. Being single is an opportunity to fall in love with the parts of you that have been overlooked by your ex.

AUGUST 1

"Heartbreak is a teacher, not a warden."

The longer you stare into the abyss of the heartbreak, the more power you give it to dictate your life. The pain is not a destination or a home—it's a teacher; it's a lesson. Use what you've learned to serve as a guide, a map, a way out.

AUGUST 2

"Embrace every bit of solitude;

discover your own magic."

S ometimes, you have to be alone to see that all the things you've
been searching for in others have been inside you the entire time.

AUGUST 3

"You're not alone in your feelings; everyone's been there."

L ooking back on my own life, I can remember those times of doubt, taking sole blame for everything that occurred. Forcing myself into this belief that I deserved all the bad things that happened. It takes time to find your way out of the mess that a breakup makes. We've all been there, struggling to see a brighter future while attempting to make sense of what happened, and while none of it comes with a road map, we use whatever it is we have within to create one. You are not alone; in fact, there are many people reading this book with you at this very moment, searching for an answer that they hold inside.

AUGUST 4

"Never fall out of self-respect because you love someone."

You will never need to compromise your self-respect to be with someone worthy of your energy, time, and love. You will never need to alter the characteristics that make you worthy of love and devotion. Stop forcing change for someone who is content with hurting you.

AUGUST 5

"In hindsight, letting go isn't losing; it's gaining the wisdom and courage to move forward."

While, initially, parting ways may seem like a major loss, in truth, it provides an opportunity to gain understanding and courage for future relationships, especially the ones in which you will be faced with the decision of moving on. By letting go, you learn that you are capable of choosing yourself when those moments come.

August 6

"To heal a wound, you eventually need
to stop touching it."

I n order to recover from painful experiences, one needs to stop
dwelling on them. The healing process often requires meditation
and or returning focus toward positive thinking, moving past the
source of the hurt.

AUGUST 7

"Every wound paints a scar, and every

scar tells a story."

Heartbreak often leaves profound emotional scars that represent moments of vulnerability, sadness, and loss, but, with time, these scars transform to begin the healing process in which they become symbols of your resilience and will to survive whatever was meant to destroy you.

AUGUST 8

"Watching from a lens of love, even pain can become a beautiful poem or painting."

In the moment, it's a wound, but in time, it becomes a story of how you conquered heartache, and in that story lie inspirations for others who are experiencing the same things you've experienced. You begin as a seed surrounded by the chaos of emotional anguish, but you grow, despite the environment, and you bloom, despite what you believed would happen to you. That's beautiful.

AUGUST 9

"Tomorrow can only begin in the way you wish when you learn how to properly let go of yesterday."

When you step into a vehicle, you instantly panic if that vehicle begins to move in reverse without end.

Don't live your life moving in reverse. You will never see the possibilities of what's ahead if you focus all of your attention on what is in your rearview mirror.

AUGUST 10

"Being single is not necessarily about being alone but being complete when by yourself."

B eing single doesn't always mean being lonely; at times, it represents self-sufficiency and completeness within oneself. It emphasizes the idea of cultivating individual fulfillment and living without requiring another person to complete one's sense of self.

AUGUST 11

"Heartbreak carves out more space inside of you for the right love."

It is often the experience that heartbreak increases one's emotional depth and capacity to love, creating a space for a more suitable and fulfilling relationship in the future. It may not feel like it at the moment, but heartbreak can expand your emotional resilience and understanding, making room for a love that's more aligned with your needs and growth.

August 12

"Happiness arrives in beautiful
waves; it comes, then goes. It'll find
you again."

Both sadness and happiness are not a constant state, but they arrive in cycles or waves, sometimes present and sometimes receding. This understanding serves as reassurance that the good you long for will always return to you, no matter how bad it gets.

AUGUST 13

"Losing someone who fails to respect you is a win."

P arting ways with an individual who doesn't show you the respect you deserve is an empowering action, not a loss. It implies that your self-respect is more important than keeping an unhealthy relationship intact.

AUGUST 14

"You are the poet of your life; don't hand the pen to anyone, especially anyone you've had to leave behind."

Take charge of your life and decisions, and do not allow others, particularly those you've distanced yourself from, to dictate your narrative or future.

AUGUST 15

"Self-love isn't vanity; it's a profound self-respect for all that you are on the inside."

Self-love is not about being narcissistic or purely focused on one's appearance but is instead about deeply respecting and appreciating your inner essence. Self-love emphasizes the importance of recognizing and valuing one's inner worth; this alone is the essence of true self-love.

August 16

"The most important thing to
remember about being happy is that
you realize you have the power to
choose what to accept and what to
let go of."

Your personal happiness is largely within your control, defined
by your choices and reactions to life's circumstances. Each and
every day, you possess the ability to choose what you embrace, such
as peace, growth, and love, and what you remove from your life, like
negativity, regrets, and toxic relationships. Every time you exercise
this power to accept and let go, you become the architect of your own
happiness.

AUGUST 17

"Relationships begin to fall apart when people stop putting in the same effort to maintain the relationship as they did in the beginning."

When a relationship begins, individuals typically invest significant energy to impress each other; doing so creates a beautiful and strong foundation, but as this effort diminishes, it causes a sense of neglect, which then creates a cycle of decay in the relationship. Only a consistent level of care can help sustain a relationship.

AUGUST 18

"Heartbreak makes you stronger; tears clean your wounds. The sadness makes you stronger."

Tears, often seen as symbols of emotional pain, also have a cleansing effect in the way they reinforce a flow into healing, paving the way to grow stronger. The sadness in your heart can fortify your emotional resilience, transforming grief into a way of understanding your ability to remain self-reliant.

AUGUST 19

"Recovery doesn't take place overnight. It is a lifelong journey that takes place one moment, one day, one step at a time."

Each moment, each day, and each step forward: Though your progression may seem small, there is great significance to what it all means on this journey. The patience you give yourself is key to weathering this storm.

August 20

"You have to stop looking at being
single as some mark against you and
realize that, in being single, it means
that you have the courage to hold out
for what you deserve."

Being single shouldn't be viewed as a negative reflection on who
you are. It is a testament to your strength and understanding of
self-worth. In a world where it's become a struggle to let go of toxic
relationships, it is important to truly comprehend the significance
of being single and preserving your heart for the right person. Being
single is not a deficiency; it's not a flaw. It's a conscious decision to
choose peace over chaos.

AUGUST 21

"Accept what has happened, let go of what-ifs, and have faith in where you're headed."

I n this journey called life, you will experience many ups, downs, and unforeseen outcomes, but it's important to lean into acceptance and let go of what-ifs. Maintain an unwavering faith in the path that lies before you.

AUGUST 22

"The pain you're feeling right now will end; maybe not now, but eventually."

During moments when your heart has been inflicted with pain, it can be difficult to envision a beautiful future, absent of struggle. However, it is important to remember that pain is never permanent and healing is a natural occurrence that unfolds over time.

How long it will take is unknown, but there can be solace in the understanding that the pain you currently feel will eventually fade into the distance.

AUGUST 23

"Whenever your heart is broken, an entryway slowly opens and gives way to a world full of new beginnings, new adventures, and new love."

Heartbreak, while it may be painful, can often serve as a cocoon for transformation. It often feels as if the ground has crumbled beneath you, placing you in the most vulnerable of places. However, amid the turmoil, a door eventually opens, revealing new possibilities, inviting you into a world of better beginnings and real love.

AUGUST 24

"The thing that breaks your heart also fixes your future."

That dreadful experience that destroyed your heart is filled with seeds of growth and newfound realizations. It holds the power to reshape and expand your future, allowing you to emerge wiser. The pain may seem like the end, but you've been here before, and you will remember how to turn these feelings into the reason you evolve.

AUGUST 25

"Remain single until you meet someone who can match the level of loyalty and devotion in your heart."

R emain single until you meet someone whose devotion resonates with your belief in what loyalty is. Someone who reciprocates the commitment you readily offer.

AUGUST 26

"Don't stay in the wrong relationship just because you've spent a lot of time and energy trying to make it work."

Don't let your ability to commit fully and or love unconditionally keep you hostage in a relationship that is fundamentally wrong for you. Understand this always: Your emotional well-being is far more important and should never be compromised due to the fear of being alone.

AUGUST 27

"Being single doesn't mean no one wants you; it means you've decided that being with someone who deserves you is far more important."

Being single doesn't mean you're undesirable. In truth, it is a message to yourself and the world that you're committed to your decision to prioritize finding a partner who will truly appreciate what it means to be with someone like you.

August 28

"Never allow your ex the opportunity
to cloud your future."

Never allow your ex's presence to distract you from the brightness that awaits in your future. Cut ties, begin healing, practice self-love, and move on. Loving yourself will ensure that their influence over your life will not overshadow the love you deserve.

August 29

"Being single is getting over the illusion that your options are endless, because you are not for everyone and everyone is not for you."

Being single is an act of liberating yourself and your heart from the misconception and lie that involves this idea of infinite choices in the realm of dating. Compatibility is rare; real love is rare. Understand that not everyone will get you, and not everyone is meant to get you. And that's okay.

AUGUST 30

"You destroy a beautiful future with someone better when you allow your ex to occupy your thoughts."

When you allow your ex to occupy your thoughts and ideas, you threaten the very existence of a beautiful future with someone who will work to prove that they are deserving of your love and presence. Release your hold on the past, be present, and open yourself up to a broader range of possibilities by letting go of those who are underserving of your touch.

AUGUST 31

"The relationships that don't work are the relationships that teach you what you need."

Each of the relationships that don't work are filled with invaluable lessons that can illuminate your future when you've successfully learned how to apply them to your life. These lessons provide a level of clarity that is so profound. They reveal to you what it takes to cultivate the type of relationship you want.

September 1

"Don't let your ex drag you

emotionally. Let go."

Exes are tricky; they often hold the key to the door you're trying
to exit from. Usually, the ones who want to keep you a prisoner
to your emotions will try to drag you down by withholding closure or
doing things to confuse your heart. Don't give them that power.

SEPTEMBER 2

"Celebrate the endings, because they open up doors to new beginnings."

All endings carry the seeds of rebirth and renewal. When a relationship ends, you are provided with a space to reflect and reassess so that you can redirect your energy to bettering your life and improving your experiences with love moving forward. Not only that, but the end is where you begin a love affair with yourself and the newfound understanding of who you truly are.

September 3

"During the process of letting go, you will lose many things that aren't meant to be carried into the future, but in doing so, you will discover more of yourself."

Sometimes, losing certain people is the pathway to a deeper understanding of your true self and paving a new road to self-discovery, personal transformation, and the freedom to embrace a future that represents the life you've been dreaming of.

SEPTEMBER 4

"If it's good, it's beautiful. If it's bad,
there's a lesson."

When a situation is unfavorable, it presents an opportunity for learning. When things are good, embrace the joy, dwell in the river of peace, and cherish every moment of it until it returns again. Every moment of your life is either to be enjoyed or to be learned from.

SEPTEMBER 5

"The toughest times of your life will always reveal the true colors of the people who claim to love you."

During the toughest times in your life, the true colors of those who claim to love you will become more evident. It's during these moments that unconditional love and support have the greatest impact, revealing to you who to keep in your life and who to let go of.

SEPTEMBER 6

"A broken heart begins to mend itself
the moment it decides to no longer
cling to the person who broke it."

When your heart gets broken, it can be extremely painful, almost to a point at which you believe you feel it physically. It hurts even more when it is due to the actions of someone you care about deeply, but it is up to you to decide to take back your power by refusing to let this person affect your feelings. Remember, anyone who wishes to harm your heart is not worthy of your mental energy.

SEPTEMBER 7

"Let it leave you if it doesn't

inspire peace."

I f you don't feel supported in your desire to remain calm and live peacefully, then it's okay to let go. There is no need to hold on to things that don't help you cultivate the peace you desire. This goes for most things, including the place you work or even your own habits. If it doesn't make you feel good, it's okay to say goodbye.

SEPTEMBER 8

"Familiar spaces are not always safe. Do not compromise your peace of mind for the familiarity of a person or place that restricts you."

There are times when the people and places we know all too well may not be the best for us. Just because you are used to something doesn't mean those interactions with it are healthy. You shouldn't compromise happiness just to stick by what you know. If a person or habit makes you feel trapped, it's okay to leave it all behind.

September 9

"Find the love you seek by first

cultivating it on your own."

Before you venture out to find love within someone else, it is important to first learn how to love yourself in all the ways you believe you need. What this means is taking care of yourself and embracing who you are. When you practice self-love, it's easier to understand whether or not you're being loved genuinely by someone else.

SEPTEMBER 10

"In the middle of a storm, there is an opportunity to cleanse your heart."

When times are tough, though difficult to manage, these are also opportunities to clear out what doesn't belong. Let go of the negative things you feel for others; set yourself free from what has been bothering you. Allow this storm to cleanse your heart and soul.

September 11

"Change is tough, but nothing is more painful than feeling stuck when your heart yearns for something more, something better."

Change can be a difficult thing to navigate, but those feelings of being stuck with no place to go can be even harder. This is always true when your heart longs for something better, something that represents what you believe you need. You have to realize that it's more painful to stay than be off on your own. When you come to terms with this, moving on will be less difficult.

SEPTEMBER 12

"You can't begin to fix the broken
pieces of your life if you're too
focused on what keeps breaking
you down."

Eventually, there will come a time when you have to seek out
solutions rather than focus on the very thing that is causing this
trouble in your heart. Fixating on past failures can often manifest an
unpleasant or undesired future. It's difficult to make a plan to resolve
things when you're consumed by everything that is wrong.

SEPTEMBER 13

"As you venture out into the world alone, avoid bringing people into your life who weigh you down."

As we walk through this journey of life and love, especially whenever we embark on new endeavors of personal growth, the people we choose to allow into our lives have a profound effect on our mindset, attitudes, and well-being. Entertaining negative people or those with cruel intentions can and will keep you from building the foundation you need to support the life you wish to lead.

SEPTEMBER 14

"The one who forgives is the one who is free to let go."

The one who is capable of forgiveness is the one who gains the opportunity to relinquish past hurt and negative emotions that cause the heart to linger in places it shouldn't. Forgiveness is the way out. Forgiveness is a vehicle that will set you free and point you in the direction of healing.

SEPTEMBER 15

"By being kinder to yourself and
patient on your journey, you invite
others to be kind and patient
toward you."

When you turn kindness and patience inward, you create a powerful precedent for how others will engage with you. By being kinder to yourself, you create a sense of self-compassion and understanding. This also shows your ability to provide these things to others, which can often bridge your life to someone who is willing to match your effort, as you are clearly demonstrating the way you wish to be loved.

SEPTEMBER 16

"When you're single, you have the opportunity to learn how it feels to be with someone like you."

While single, you welcome the opportunity to intimately understand who you are, gaining a level of insight that is priceless. You begin to understand how it feels for someone to be with someone like you. In doing so, you learn what areas need improvement within yourself. In truth, being single offers a transformative period when you are present enough to develop insight on how you want your future relationship to be by becoming the type of person you want to be with.

SEPTEMBER 17

"True love is a journey that often
begins at the end of a relationship."

I think real love should be treated like an expedition that often begins after the conclusion of a previous relationship. In the end, you are provided many lessons that will prepare you for a deeper and more fulfilling connection in the future. At the end of a relationship is when you will uncover things that will help your next relationship thrive.

SEPTEMBER 18

"Nothing about you is ordinary. Please don't settle for mediocrity."

You are unique—rare, in many ways. It just takes time to see yourself for all that you are. You have a profound potential to be someone capable of cultivating a beautiful and lasting story of love, but you will find in your life that not everyone you meet on this journey will be able to appreciate the essence of your existence, and while that's fine, it will still hurt because you desire to be seen in a way that makes your heart rejoice. Though it may be tempting to settle because you're tired of being alone or getting it wrong, never put the rare diamond that is your heart in hands that refuse to see its value.

September 19

"Relationships are about empowering one another, not having power over one another."

An ideal relationship should be empowering, in which both individuals are in full support of each other's desire to grow and maintain autonomy and self-confidence. Relationships are not to be made to fuel the need to dominate or control the other person. Relationships thrive on a power that is equally shared and a mutual focus on both individuals flourishing and being at peace.

SEPTEMBER 20

"Maintain the courage to trust new love when old love is not strong enough to go on."

I t takes pure resilience to embrace new love when past loves have wilted like roses losing life. It's scary to trust once more in the power of love when your heart has had its share of pain, but there is a reward in deciding not to allow your past to dictate a future filled with everything you deserve.

September 21

"Stop waiting for someone else to do
what you've been capable of doing
this entire time."

R ight now, you're holding yourself back by waiting for someone
else to take an action that you are perfectly capable of doing on
your own. By understanding what you are truly capable of, you are
free to initiate the changes your heart needs.

SEPTEMBER 22

"In a world where it's so easy to fall for pretty words, pay more attention to actions."

In a world where the heart is often manipulated by charming lies, it is important to judge someone's heart and intentions by the things they do rather than by what is said. We've all been there, easily swooned by a lie because that lie represented everything we've always wanted to hear. You must understand that words can be twisted to form sentences that seem beautiful, but if those words do not align with what is being done, then it is completely okay to stop listening.

SEPTEMBER 23

"Assumptions destroy the potential of a beautiful future. Always seek clarity, and remember that you alone can provide the answers you need."

Don't assume it's love because it's been hinted to be. Don't assume there's a future when it hasn't been discussed. Don't make assumptions in place of what has been shown to you all out of fear of something falling short of what you believe it could be. Too often, we focus on the potential of a person, and we assume that they are capable of becoming the person we think they can become. Don't assume that it is more than it is or that they can be more than they are willing to be.

SEPTEMBER 24

"You stop waiting for someone to give you flowers when you discover the ability to plant and nurture your own garden."

You ou stop waiting for the sky to lift the sun when you discover your own light. You stop waiting for summer when you understand that there is a beautiful and wild warmth living within you. You stop chasing love when you realize that you walk with it because it exists inside your heart. You stop waiting for the rain when you discover the ability to water yourself. Stop waiting for others to be what you already are.

SEPTEMBER 25

"The only love to live desperately for is
the love that comes from within."

The love that originates from within is worthy of your attention.
You've been fighting for people who do not have the strength
to fight for you, neglecting yourself to run after those who refuse
to acknowledge your efforts. And while it may hurt to imagine a
life alone, it is important to understand that a life alone offers you a
chance to see a soul mate: you.

September 26

"You are not what happened to you. In truth, you are what you decide to be in the aftermath of what hurt your heart."

You are not the damage in your heart; you are not solely defined by the things or events that have caused you emotional anguish. You are more than a product of your past and or the relationships that had no chance of working out. It's hard to see yourself as more when your heart is hurting, but you will discover that how you choose to react and move forward will determine who you are and what you're made of.

SEPTEMBER 27

"In loss, we gain. In hurt, we grow. The pain is a blessing. We learn the most from what hurts the most."

Within every loss is an unexpected chance to gain. The loss is often a blessing in disguise, for we are blessed with the chance to reroute our lives and place ourselves on the right path. You were going the wrong way; the hurt you feel will lead you in the right direction. Be patient with yourself.

SEPTEMBER 28

"Do not allow yourself to be treated like a worthless stone when you have always been a diamond."

The way your ex perceives you should not be a determining factor of your value. And just because they couldn't appreciate the rare gem that is your heart doesn't mean no one ever will. You are precious and unique, and you will only need to know it for it to be true.

SEPTEMBER 29

"When you begin to evolve to your
highest self, you only lose people who
wish you to remain stuck in a place
that is too small to hold your heart."

The only relationships you run the risk of losing on your journey
of evolving to your highest self are the ones that represent a
means to keeping you distracted or stuck in your old ways. You will
come to understand that the wrong relationships tend to confine
you to a version of yourself that you don't wish to be or keep you in
emotional limbo, experiencing things you no longer wish to feel. It's
natural to outgrow certain relationships, especially the ones that no
longer serve you or support the way you are meant to live. When you
lose these relationships, you make room for something better.

SEPTEMBER 30

"Do not abandon who you are in order
to be the person they want you to be
when, in truth, the person you are
is just too much for them to truly
comprehend."

You do not need to fit someone else's expectations and or desired image of who you are to be deserving of love. Especially if that idea of you causes you to compromise the very things that make you beautiful and courageous from within. It's important to fully understand that if someone fails to appreciate the depth of who you are, it is not a reflection of your self-worth but rather a clear indication of their limited capacity to appreciate the richness and beauty that you represent.

OCTOBER 1

"Simplicity is love. The more you let go of, the closer you are to a life that welcomes a love that resembles freedom."

The less emotional clutter you have, the more space you make for the right type of love to occupy spaces in your heart. The more you remove what doesn't belong, the easier it is for you to belong to you and possibly someone who will appreciate the space you've provided for them. Love doesn't need to be complicated. Love doesn't have to be a mess.

OCTOBER 2

"Self-love is often labeled as selfishness from those who wish to keep you blind to the power you hold within."

S elf-love can often be misidentified as being selfish, but, in truth, it is a powerful tool that is best used for self-empowerment. Self-love can feel threatening to people who do not want you to figure out that you are good enough on your own and that you have everything you need without them in your life. When someone sees your ability to honor yourself as an issue, take this as a sign of bad intentions. Self-love is an awakening to the love you are capable of giving yourself and the love that you are to expect from others.

OCTOBER 3

"Stop sitting at tables that do not serve
the honesty and devotion you need."

Never linger in spaces where the honesty and devotion you seek is nonexistent. These elements of character are both vital in the success of a relationship. Remember, sometimes you have to step away so that you can step into the love you need.

OCTOBER 4

"Owning what you deserve and deciding to walk away even while you love that person with all your heart is the bravest thing you can do."

The decision to walk away from a relationship with a loved one that is no longer supporting your needs is a tough choice to make, but it's also very brave to go without the things you want in order to get closer to all the things you need. In doing so, you find that the person to truly invest your energy into is yourself. This decision asserts self-respect and gives you the opportunity to cultivate a beautiful foundation on which real love can be built.

OCTOBER 5

"Sometimes, you have to get out of love so that real love can be allowed into your life."

Walking away makes room for a more authentic and rewarding love. Sometimes, the "love" you've settled for can block the entryway of the love of your dreams making an entrance into your life. Letting go is often an act of opening yourself up to a deeper, more profound connection.

OCTOBER 6

"Sometimes, the love you planned is
not the love that is waiting for you."

L ife has a way of surprising you in terms of discovering something
beautiful. These surprises are presented as a version of love that
is unexpected. Though some of these experiences are different from
your original plans, you find that what is presented to you is more
rewarding and more beautiful than your wildest dreams. Letting go of
the wrong person keeps your heart open for such experiences.

OCTOBER 7

"In order to step into a beautiful and
bright future, you must first come
to terms with the belief that your
dark past is no longer worthy of your
mental energy."

Your past no longer deserves your mental energy. When you realize that nothing in the past can be changed and that what lies behind you is out of your control, you can finally begin the process of moving forward with your life. When you release the urge to focus on the painful things that happened to you, you are free to embrace the beautiful possibilities of a future that resembles things that will fill your heart with joy and your mind with peace. You have to come to terms with the fact that everything that happened to you was also happening for you.

OCTOBER 8

"You are free to leave when the pain
of staying is greater than the pain of
being on your own."

You are welcome to walk out of a relationship if the pain of staying outweighs the pain of being alone. It is this feeling that makes the transition easier to bear. I often think that it is difficult to exit a relationship when the fear of being on one's own is much greater than being with the wrong person. In time, you get there; in your own time, you experience whatever is needed to help you foster the courage to walk in the opposite direction. It's natural to be afraid of leaving behind what is familiar, but you have to make peace with severing ties with anyone who makes love seem chaotic.

October 9

"So many people lose themselves
while fighting for people who do not
care about losing them."

D o not lose your sense of self, fighting for the love of someone who is indifferent to your wants and needs. The energy you invest in doing so is detrimental to the courage it takes to leave the wrong person. I sometimes think that the people who push you to compromise yourself are aware of what they're doing. When you lose yourself, it is that much harder to leave because you've forgotten that you have always been able to surpass the things that no longer fit into your life.

OCTOBER 10

"When you learn to enjoy being alone, you are less likely to settle for the presence of people who tear you down."

When you learn to enjoy solitude, you reduce your tolerance for anything that is harmful to the life you wish to lead. When you are able to find genuine comfort in your own presence, you are less inclined to settle for people who mistreat you.

OCTOBER 11

"They miss you, but they were the
reason for the distance. They love
you, but often you felt hated. They're
sorry but rarely apologized when you
needed that the most."

It's funny how the person expressing a desire for your presence is the same person who chose to do the very things that would push you out of their lives. That same person proclaims their love for you, despite spending the majority of the relationship causing you to feel hated. They're filled with regret and apologies only after they neglected to own up to all the moments that destroyed your self-esteem and altered your belief in love. Remember this when they attempt to reenter your life as if nothing ever happened.

OCTOBER 12

"You're single because you're willing
to preserve your heart for a love that
doesn't get tired of being loved."

I t's important to understand that being single is not to be associated with being inadequate. It is a beautiful and profound proclamation of your desire to safeguard your heart against negativity. Being single is a choice to remain available for the right love.

OCTOBER 13

"Demand what you deserve, but understand your own capability of meeting your own demands."

Understanding your ability to meet the demands of your heart is paramount. It is just as important as what you expect from others. With this understanding, you establish healthy boundaries with would-be partners while also acknowledging and strengthening your self-sufficiency.

OCTOBER 14

"Healthy relationships are built upon trust and transparency, not promises."

Promises can be broken. Promises can be used as manipulation. Promises can easily mirror the desires of people with no true intent of actually following through with what is being proclaimed. Relationships should be grounded upon foundations built by trust and transparency. This is how you create strong and enduring connections.

OCTOBER 15

"You are everything you'll ever need.
Right now, you are the love of
your life."

Y ou embody everything you need. In the moment of you reading these words, you are the love of your life, and you are fully capable of providing yourself with respect, love, and the care you deserve.

OCTOBER 16

"Better single than taken for granted."

Being overlooked in a relationship compromises your self-worth, and without self-worth, you remain in the wrong relationship for longer periods of time. The longer you remain in those relationships, the harder it is to move on. It is better to embrace the single life rather than lend your life's energy to someone who can't comprehend the beauty and brilliance that is you and the blessing you can be in their life.

OCTOBER 17

"It wasn't love. Just heavy

manipulation."

Sometimes, manipulation is disguised as affection. Genuine love is uplifting; it's supportive and is symbolic of respect. What you experienced was something resembling exploitation; it was a relationship built on deception. And every time you decided to open up with how they made you feel, they decided to belittle those feelings.

OCTOBER 18

"I'm not sorry for wanting what I deserve, and I'm not afraid to walk away to find it."

There will be no reason to apologize for wanting what you deserve, nor for having the conviction and the courage to walk away in search of something that makes your heart swell with happiness. This is a testament of your desire to live happily and peacefully in the presence of someone who is eager to do the same.

OCTOBER 19

"A love that doesn't break under the
weight of an argument is what I
desire; it's what I deserve."

A love that is built on communication. A love that is filled with
understanding, a desire to not only express one's side but
to also actively listen to the other. A relationship that doesn't fold
beneath a difference of opinion. This level of understanding is an
essential ingredient for what makes a relationship work.

OCTOBER 20

"Sometimes, you have to choose badly in order to be able to identify what is good for you."

Sometimes, in order to know what is truly beneficial to you and your life, you have to make the wrong choices. This is a necessary step in figuring out the difference between what you want, what you deserve, and what you need.

Though at times difficult, these experiences will always guide you down the path of understanding how to make the right decisions regarding your future.

OCTOBER 21

"One day, you won't be waiting for them. One day, you'll be able to think of them and smile, knowing you dodged a bullet."

The day will come when your heart no longer searches for a feeling inspired by a person who was no longer worth your energy. A day will come when you won't be waiting for them to become the person they promised they'd be. You will look back on that relationship and rejoice because the ending of it was a blessing in disguise.

OCTOBER 22

"The secret of letting go is realizing
that you're worthy of the type of love
they're unable to provide."

Wwhen you are in full acceptance of the fact that they were incapable of loving you properly, you will be free to release the hold of past relationships with people who could not meet your standards in terms of the love your heart requires.

OCTOBER 23

"You've been fighting for their love
and affection for so long that you've
forgotten how to love yourself."

It's time to redirect your energy toward nurturing the garden that is your heart. You've spent entirely too much time seeking out love and validation from the wrong person. In doing this, you have forgotten the way to your heart. I hope you know that it is never too late to return to yourself. It is never too late to find the missing piece that is you.

OCTOBER 24

"I am enough, just not for you."

Repeat this whenever you suffer beneath the weight of thinking you're not good enough. "I am enough, just not for you." You have always been enough, and it's okay if the people you love just don't get it. You are a puzzle piece that isn't meant to be the perfect fit for just anyone. When you don't fit into someone's life, it doesn't diminish your worth. It's just that sometimes we allow our needs to take us down a wrong path. It is there where we discover the pain that comes from being incompatible with another person.

OCTOBER 25

"You deserve the world, even if it

means giving it to yourself."

Recognizing your own worth is the first step toward ensuring that you receive all the love, respect, and peace you deserve. The realization that you can give all of this to yourself is a beautiful gift; not only that, it's vital as you walk through life alone, free and available for the right things.

OCTOBER 26

"Truth is, you're not okay, but you will be. You'll hold on, but then you'll let go. It'll be difficult, but you'll do it. You're feeling weak, but be strong."

You'll endure everything that hurts, and, eventually, you will set yourself free. This journey will always be difficult, but you will find a way to persevere. Even as you feel broken or weak, your courage will reveal itself, and your strength will eventually shine through and give direction to what path you must take.

OCTOBER 27

"You were enough. Maybe you were
too much. Maybe they prefer less, and
you deserve more."

These is just a reminder that you were always enough. You come
equipped with a magic in your heart that makes you a rare
being, but, even so, you will find yourself in relationships with people
who do not see you for all that you are. But your value isn't defined
by those who would rather turn a blind eye than experience the full
glory and radiance that is your heart and the love you have to offer.

OCTOBER 28

"Keep revisiting your past and you'll
never make it to the future."

The cycle of revisiting your past is too harmful of a risk to take. You stall your progression toward a brighter future. While the past may hold lessons and be littered with valuable information, don't let it slow you down just to look in a direction that no longer deserves your gaze.

OCTOBER 29

"I forgive my past; I forgive who I
used to be."

The easiest way to practice self-liberation is in the forgiveness
of the mistakes you've made in the past. You have to make
peace with who you were so that you can become the person you're
meant to be.

OCTOBER 30

"You still cared; you only walked away because you realized they didn't."

The decision to leave wasn't due to some lack of affection. In all honesty, you still cared. There was still love inside your heart. It's their lack of affection that gave you no choice but to choose yourself.

OCTOBER 31

"Five years from now, they'll be

nothing more than a memory. Don't

let them destroy you."

Don't allow this temporary chapter of your life do significant and permanent damage to your future.

November 1

"There is always a message in the way someone treats you. Open your heart, and listen to what you feel."

Pay attention to the way people interact with you, especially the person you might want to entertain a relationship with. This is where the narrative of their true intentions and feelings will often be told in fullness. A lot of the truth you seek will come in the form of nonverbal dialogue that can rival anything that anyone could say. By remaining in tune with how you feel, you are fully receptive to the truth of what is happening and who someone truly is.

November 2

"Let it hurt, then let it go."

When you experience the anguish of a situation, allow it to wash over you, but also let those feelings pass through you so that they can run their course. Listen, it's not going to always be easy, but allow yourself to feel every bit of pain so that you can discover a way out of it.

NOVEMBER 3

"It's as simple as this: You just want what you give."

That desire to receive the same degree of kindness and effort you pour into others is a natural feeling. There is nothing wrong with wanting to be in the company of people who share in some of the same actions and energy that make you feel safe and loved. It is vital in one's life to entertain people who are capable of mirroring the right type of energy, not just because you deserve it but because this is the way to create powerful bonds that help both parties grow in the most beautiful of ways. Life is too short to settle for a relationship that isn't equipped to handle the love and respect you require.

NOVEMBER 4

"Even at your worst, you are fucking
incredible."

Despite those moments of failure and struggle, your self-worth
remains intact. All those moments of difficulty in your life
don't devalue you.

Remember always that, despite the low points, you are capable
of remaining powerful. You are incredibly brave. You are a brilliant
light during your darkest moments and always capable of doing
extraordinary things.

NOVEMBER 5

"You're too good for someone who isn't sure about you."

To the person reading these words, I want you to understand that your self-worth is not contingent upon someone's unwillingness to see you for who you are. You have to understand and lean into this idea of deserving something that is unwavering and full of affection that will make your heart smile. Any relationship you enter should reflect a mutual level of appreciation.

NOVEMBER 6

"You're going to date a few cowards
before you meet someone brave
enough to love you."

The search for real love will involve many encounters with people who will not be readily prepared to commit to you and or help you cultivate the type of relationship you long for. There will also be people who will seek out your desire for something real and use your longing as a foundation to manipulate you into making spaces in your heart that they were never willing to work for. Sadly, the journey to finding a mate will lead you down many dead ends. Some will be a waste of time while others will offer up a few lessons as you continue forward. Despite this, you will need to remain patient because, eventually, you will meet someone who possesses the courage to love you surely and deeply.

November 7

"Knowing the difference between what you want and what you need is key to finding genuine love."

The only way to discover and maintain a relationship that brings you genuine love is to understand the difference between your wants and needs. Wants are usually rooted in the superficial and remain on surface level, but your needs dwell where the eyes can't see. In understanding the difference, you are able to discern whether or not the relationship you've chosen to entertain is one in which genuine love can thrive.

NOVEMBER 8

"There's nothing romantic about
losing someone to someone else
only for that person to return to you
because they failed at replacing you
with someone else."

The action of someone you loved returning to you after a failed attempt at creating a better connection with someone else is not a romantic notion. In truth, it is a reflection of their complete and utter disrespect for your feelings and the relationship you were both a part of. It serves as proof that they do not value the effort you've invested, as they were willing to lose you due to their belief that you were not good enough. They will, in fact, return because they will have realized that you alone were everything they could ever want, but you will not allow them back in because, by then, you will have realized that when you gave them your all, they made it seem as if it were nothing.

NOVEMBER 9

"Love isn't stupid; you just keep loving stupid people."

It's easy to believe that the love you desire is simply a fantasy due to the fact that is hasn't been easy to find, but you must understand that love in itself isn't foolish, and it shouldn't be seen as a fool's errand. When we repeatedly invest in people who do not value us, our sense of love can become warped. We begin to believe that what we expect is just too much to ask for. We mistake the unworthiness of the people we date as an indication that real love is some stupid idea or an impossible feeling to cultivate. It's not love that is wrong, it's not love that is foolish, it's the choice of the people we choose to love.

NOVEMBER 10

"You are something wonderful, and
every day, you happen to yourself."

Each and every day, you are a miracle unfolding and expanding,
stretching out, taking up space. You are a beautiful blending
of strength, weaknesses, passions, and wisdom. Each and every day,
you get to experience the brilliant miracle that is you. All that you
are, even in times of distress, is what makes you unique and powerful.
Embrace yourself today. Give yourself the love you seek.

NOVEMBER 11

"Love without compromising the peace in your heart."

L ove should add peace to your life; the love you allow into your heart should be wrapped in tranquility and kindness. It is vital, maintaining a sense of inner peace and refusing to allow your love for someone to disrupt the natural order of the joy and serenity that you are cultivating. Love with all your heart, but not at the cost of your peace of mind.

November 12

"Some people can't find the words
to describe their pain, and so they
just claim to be fine while breaking
from within."

It's natural to mask the truth of what you feel by claiming to be okay when, in truth, you are falling apart at the seams. There is nothing more painful than being able to articulate the feelings of dread in your soul. You bear so much of your pain in silence, unable to find the words, and maybe you're reading this now with a heavy heart, holding back tears, longing to be seen . . . I SEE YOU.

NOVEMBER 13

"Stop giving your heart to someone who only ever wants your body."

Refrain from sharing your whole heart with someone who is only interested in being physical. While you are free to do as you please, never let anyone believe that you are nothing but a body when you are so much more.

November 14

"Imagine someone loving you
just as much as you've loved the
wrong people."

Take a moment to envision being cherished by someone as deeply as you've once loved those who were never worthy of your devotion. You've given a love so deep, freely; imagine receiving that level of affection. Imagine a love that matches the intensity of what lies in your heart. Now, give that love to yourself.

NOVEMBER 15

"Stop searching for healing in the same relationship that hurt your soul."

Searching for healing in the relationship that broke you is a waste of emotional energy. Do not look for a cure in the same place that harmed you. The relationship that destroyed you is not a space of redemption.

r.h. Sin

NOVEMBER 16

"When trust is broken, everything said
after sounds like a lie."

When trust is broken, the words that follow a betrayal are laced
with doubt. Promises become empty shells, explanations
begin to mirror excuses, and a sincere gesture feels more like
manipulation. Broken trust taints love and every interaction that
follows, making it nearly impossible to repair. Be honest, be faithful,
and demand that the person you've given your heart to does the same,
and if they are unwilling, leave. Do not spend the rest of your life
holding on to relationships that drain you of life and keep you living
what feels like a lie.

NOVEMBER 17

"I hope you find someone who
understands how to love you at your
most broken."

E ven in the devastation of your heart, you are deserving of a love
that is kind and doesn't distract you from the work needed
to begin healing. May you discover a love that doesn't go missing
when your heart is hurting or unable to experience the joy it requires.
May you encounter someone who isn't afraid to love your most
fractured state of being. Someone who can see your brokenness for
the beautiful story it can be. Someone able to nurture and foster a
safe and trusting place by putting in the necessary work. This is my
wish for you.

NOVEMBER 18

"You have suffered enough. It's time

to thrive."

You've always been able to endure the suffering, no matter how painful. So much so that it is finally time for you to rise above the things that were meant to destroy you. You have been a survivor your entire life, and it's time to thrive.

NOVEMBER 19

"Don't be the person they can return to after leaving you to be with someone else."

After becoming an afterthought, do not allow your ex to make you a secondary option for when the relationship they abandoned you for doesn't work out the way they thought it would. Maintain your self-respect by choosing yourself over someone who refused to choose you.

NOVEMBER 20

"It hurts to be overlooked and
neglected. You just want to make
sense to someone who is prepared to
love you the way you deserve."

R ight now, all you really want is to find someone who recognizes
your worth without putting you through hell. Someone who
cherishes you with a love that matches the love you've given to others
and the love you've given to yourself. This is what the pain of being
overlooked does to a person. It leaves you longing for someone who
truly understands you and loves you in the way you deserve.

NOVEMBER 21

"The only problem with being kind
is that, oftentimes, you find yourself
trying harder for people who were
never worth your energy."

The problem with kindness is that you find yourself sharing it with people who either don't appreciate it or reciprocate it. The challenge lies in the realization that everything you did went unnoticed. You can't continue to give to people who believe you deserve nothing. Be kind, but do not allow yourself to be a doormat. You have to stop allowing people the opportunity to use your kindness against you. Remember, you are not obligated to be soft toward people who make it seem as if you're too hard to care for.

November 22

"I will never be sorry for wanting more than you were willing to give. I will never apologize for knowing that I deserved more than you expected me to settle for."

Knowing your worth and refusing to settle for less is something that you should always protect and stand by without regret. Never apologize for desiring a love that is aligned with the level of love you're capable of giving.

NOVEMBER 23

"'It's easier said than done' is not an excuse to continue entertaining the wrong relationship."

Naturally, just because a relationship is harmful doesn't mean it's easy to end. The phrase 'it's easier said than done,' though factual, should not be used to justify staying in a toxic relationship.

Acknowledging the need for change is the first step toward setting yourself free.

NOVEMBER 24

"The moment you stop chasing the
wrong person, you give yourself
an opportunity at more self-love
and healing."

The act of freeing yourself from the wrong person allows you the chance to redirect your energy toward personal growth and discovering genuine connections in a world filled with fraudulent behavior. When you refrain from pursuing someone who isn't right for you, you open yourself up to self-love and the chance to work on healing your wounds.

NOVEMBER 25

"I hope you find the courage to be comfortable with being alone. This is how you heal yourself. By finding solitude, away from all the people who hurt you."

May your heart discover its ability to remain brave as it looks to embrace solitude and find peace in being alone. For this is the path toward true healing. Stepping in the opposite direction of the people who caused you pain enables you to prioritize your well-being and health of your heart.

November 26

"Cancel this idea of holding on to someone who gives you a 'love' that feels like hate."

Release yourself from this all-too-familiar toxic cycle of accepting a love that causes you pain. Reject the action of clinging to someone who disguises their mistreatment and neglect as love. Their actions are rooted in manipulation and negativity. You deserve better; you deserve more.

November 27

"Being able to fully love someone even after you've been hurt shows courage, not weakness."

It is an act of courage, opening your heart up again, even when it's been wounded numerous times before. Loving someone with your whole heart despite experiencing hurt is a display of remarkable emotional strength and resilience. Loving someone like you've never been hurt is beautiful; it's not a weakness.

November 28

"Stop dumbing yourself down to be in a relationship that will never live up to your emotional expectations."

Your authenticity is beautiful; embrace it. Seek out connections with which your emotional expectations are fulfilled and the energy you give is matched. Stop suppressing your true self and your heart's desires to maintain a lukewarm relationship that falls short of meeting your emotional needs.

November 29

"When the calls come, don't answer.

When the text arrives, don't respond."

R esist all temptation to interact when the person who hurt your heart tries to reach out to a place they no longer should be able to access. By refusing to answer, you reclaim your power, and you send a message that you are ready to prioritize your emotional well-being while preparing yourself for better experiences. Focus on yourself; your ex has nothing meaningful to show you.

November 30

"Sometimes, that person has to lose you to fully comprehend your worth. Once you walk away, never go back."

Isn't it unfortunate the way that some people only realize your true worth when they no longer have access to you? And in those instances, it is essential to decline their requests for another chance to potentially waste your time. Once you have built up the courage and strength to move forward, it's crucial to stay committed to your decision to want more for yourself and not less of what you deserve.

DECEMBER 1

"One day, they'll look back and regret losing someone with a heart like yours. By then, you'll have figured out how to bloom in their absence."

Eventually, those who decided to overlook the love in your heart will be weighed down with the regret of losing a genuine and profound love; by then, you will have learned to thrive, heal, and maintain love in their absence. It is when you are without the people who made you feel unappreciated that you rediscover your ability to blossom independent of their presence.

December 2

"There is nothing wrong with detaching yourself from people who would rather see you in pain."

When you prioritize your well-being, you create healthy boundaries by putting distance between yourself and toxic influences. It is perfectly acceptable to choose detachment from people who feel a sense of satisfaction seeing you in pain.

DECEMBER 3

"There is salvation in the emptiness left behind by the people who were not brave enough to fight for a spot in your heart."

The emptiness left in your heart is created by those who lacked the confidence to reside there. Those people didn't have the courage to fight for a place in your heart. That absence allows space for new possibilities and opportunities to find what your heart identifies as genuine.

December 4

"In order to heal, you must move forward without the people who hurt you. In order to love yourself, you must find the courage to move on from relationships that cause you to compromise your peace of mind."

Self-love is the author of cultivating a level of courage that enables you to let go of relationships that require you to compromise your inner peace. Healing will require you to rid yourself of anyone who makes you feel like the love you deserve is an impossible dream. It's easy to mistake the void that will be left as a hole of misery, but, in truth, that space, the one that feels empty at first, is really a vehicle of inner peace. You protect it by letting go.

DECEMBER 5

"Self-care is about detaching from relationships that are unhealthy. Self-care is about removing the wrong people from your life."

In the practice of self-care, you must avoid any relationship that is detrimental to your emotional and mental health. Take a moment to figure out who in your life is the reason for the pain you feel, and begin the process of removing the idea of them from your future plans. When you recognize the importance of removing the wrong people from your life, you increase the chances of leaving room for positivity, peace, and a love that feels beautiful.

DECEMBER 6

"Being with the wrong person means more loneliness in your heart. You lose nothing when you lose people who neglect you."

Y ou deepen the sense of loneliness in your heart when you choose to hold on to the person who has proven to be wrong for you time and time again. Losing those who have no respect for your heart is not an actual loss, as it breathes life into your personal freedom and welcomes something beautiful to occur in your life. The wrong person will never be able to get it right because they're not meant to. Letting go is how you begin to reward your heart. Letting go is how you discover the prize. Stop giving energy to people who want you to neglect your future by sharing your presence with them.

DECEMBER 7

"'I miss you' text messages are a way to manipulate a lonely heart. Ignore them."

"I miss you" text messages are a modern-day manipulation tactic to take control over a broken heart. The person who usually sends these messages is often the reason the relationship ended and is aware of the fact that they are preying upon someone who is vulnerable and lonely. Protect yourself from those who should not be allowed back into your life.

DECEMBER 8

"Something better will happen,

someone better will come along,

but until then, pour into yourself

whatever it is you need to feel

loved again."

H ave faith in this idea that there is something better awaiting you in the future and with someone who will truly work to prove that they are deserving of a place next to you in this life. In the meantime, focus on cultivating self-love and nurturing the garden in your heart with the love you deserve. Understand that you are capable of filling your own cup and quenching your own thirst for love. Give yourself to you until the right person arrives.

DECEMBER 9

"Waiting around for them to change is

a waste of your heart."

Investing your heart's energy into hoping that someone will change is a waste of time that hurts your own mental health.

Give your energy back to yourself by investing it in improving yourself and meeting someone who loves you for who you are.

DECEMBER 10

"No matter how difficult this becomes, you are strong enough to survive this ache in your heart. This pain will not keep you from the love you deserve."

Remind yourself today that you are strong and resilient. Think back to all the things you've had to overcome in your life, knowing that you have the power to get through the pain that is in your heart. Believe that this pain will not keep you from finding the love, peace, and happiness that you deserve.

DECEMBER 11

"Your scars tell stories of how often

you've gone to war and survived.

Don't hide them; don't be ashamed."

E very wound, every scar has borne witness to the emotional wars
you've had to face and conquer, serving as true testaments to
your strength.

Wear them proudly; embrace your scars, for they are a part of
your victory over everything that has brought pain into your heart.

DECEMBER 12

"It's so much harder to believe in
a joyful love when what you've
often settled for is a love that
resembles hell."

I know that it can become difficult to have faith in a love that
brings you solace when you have experienced a love that resembles
emotional torment and unnecessary suffering, but by taking a
moment to recognize the difference and refusing to settle, you open
yourself up to something that you, at times, believe to be impossible.

December 13

"Focus on your goals; most of the people you meet will only want to waste your time."

Make sure to turn your focus toward your goals and aspirations, as many people you encounter may only want to serve as distractions in your life. Prioritize the elevation of your life, and surround yourself with people who are in full support of your desire to grow into everything you're meant to be.

December 14

"A love that doesn't remind you of pain.
A love that doesn't turn into a lie. A
love that isn't easily fractured by a
disagreement."

S eek out a love that doesn't trigger those familiar feelings of pain.
A love that remains truthful and that is capable of withstanding
disagreement without falling apart so easily. Strive to create a loving
space where peace can dwell, where both parties remain authentic
without fear of being judged. This is how you create a resilient
relationship.

DECEMBER 15

"There will come a time when you begin to place higher importance on who deserves to be with you rather than who simply wants to be with you."

Eventually, it'll happen; you will finally reach a point where you are ready to prioritize those who are deserving of a space in your life over those who merely express a lukewarm desire to be with you. Remember: quality over quantity.

DECEMBER 16

"Sometimes, you don't actually miss that person. Sometimes, you just miss the echo of everything they used to pretend to be."

You know what, sometimes the longing you feel for that person isn't about the actual person but the illusion you believed in. There was a need in your life, and they arrived, only to play a part that was never rooted in truth. Understand that missing that person may simply be a result of missing the lie rather than their genuine self.

December 17

"Love itself never has to be perfect, but it also doesn't have to hurt so bad."

L ove need not be faultless, but it should never be so painful that its recipients can't bear it.

Try to find a love that brings you happiness, growth, and satisfaction instead of suffering.

DECEMBER 18

"A relationship shouldn't be about
surviving the person you're with."

I t must be hard when all you wanted was to be loved, but instead you're stuck in a constant limbo, confused about how to feel, wasting away in your devotion for someone who doesn't care for your heart. Each day feels like a battle that you are meant to lose, forced to fight for your life, fighting for a love that is nonexistent. A healthy relationship shouldn't revolve around merely surviving the person who should instead be protecting your heart and providing a safe space for you to express the truth in how you feel.

DECEMBER 19

"Stop giving second chances to people
who never appreciated the first."

B reak the unhealthy cycle of granting second chances to those
who failed to appreciate the initial opportunity to protect your
heart. Value yourself enough to be able to recognize that the person
searching for a way back into your life is the person who is no longer
worthy of trust and has always acted in some of the most disloyal
ways. When someone shows you just how easy it is for them to
choose to lose you, let them stay gone.

December 20

"You deserve someone who won't force you to compete with the screen on their phone. You deserve someone who won't force you to compete with the people they follow on social media. You deserve someone who doesn't turn love into a contest."

You deserve a partner who places a higher importance on your presence and values real-life connection over the distractions of a virtual space. Choose a partner who respects and cherishes you without making you feel like you come second or have to compete for their attention and affection.

DECEMBER 21

"The more you fall for yourself, the more you fall out of love with things that no longer serve and protect you."

As you begin to develop a deeper love and appreciation for the person staring back at you in the mirror, you naturally begin to recognize and let go of anything that no longer supports your overall well-being. The moment you fall in love with yourself, you enhance the power to prioritize your focus on all the things that protect your peace of mind and your belief in happiness.

December 22

"Stay away from people who claim they're not ready for a relationship but expect you to be fully committed to them."

Beware of the people who will use this idea of not being ready for a relationship as an excuse not to commit to you while also demanding your unwavering devotion and loyalty. You have to protect yourself from these people by avoiding those who are not willing to meet you halfway and or honor your emotional needs. If you want more, if you want something real, communicate this and walk away from anyone who thinks it best for you to settle for their version of good enough.

DECEMBER 23

"You may never forget them, but you will find a way to survive without them because, while it may not feel like it, you are capable of giving your heart whatever it needs."

E ven while it may be impossible to fully erase someone from your mind, you do possess the ability and strength to move forward without them. Remember this: You have the power to provide your heart with the love and care it has always deserved, especially in their absence.

I honestly hate this idea of you giving the best parts of yourself to someone who can't even comprehend what you are, and I genuinely hope you're reading every word and applying these ideas to your life, because you are special, and you deserve a love that reflects that. You are capable of giving this love to yourself.

December 24

"You have to stop choosing heartache over joy. You have to stop choosing sleepless nights over rest. You have to stop choosing the person who has chosen to fight you instead of for you."

Pursue joy; remain open to the possibilities of bliss. Do whatever it is you need to cultivate peace in your life. It's time to break the pattern of willingly subjecting your heart to pain. Choose sleep over the restless nights of thinking about someone who doesn't think about you. Free yourself from the conflict of trying to fight for someone who would rather fight against you.

DECEMBER 25

"You are the gift; you've always been.

Take yourself out of hands that fail to

appreciate you."

R emove yourself from the grasp of those who fail to honor and appreciate the precious gift that is your heart. You do this by understanding and defining your own worth. You know how it feels to be loved by you through acts of self-love. Protect that energy. Choose only to be in relationships in which your value is celebrated.

DECEMBER 26

"Stop reaching for the person you've
been trying to save yourself from."

Fighting for the approval or love of someone who has often been a source of trauma and self-doubt is a painful thing to do to one's heart. Your desire for them is a contradiction to self-love and the protection that you deserve. Don't undermine your longing for love by turning your focus toward someone incapable of loving you.

DECEMBER 27

"Solitude is a gift, being alone is the reward, and being single a chance to figure out what you need outside of yourself to feel safe, respected, and loved."

I can't stress this enough: Solitude is a beautiful opportunity. Being alone is a prize, the solitude is a reward, and being single provides more chances to determine what external factors you will need to feel secure, loved, and respected. I know that being single can get so lonely, but if you surrender to those moments, you will find the freedom to experience the greatest love that is your own.

December 28

"You're not running from your troubles.
You've simply decided to stop
facing things that are better off left
behind you."

You aren't escaping your problems, despite popular belief to the contrary. What you've done is made a calculated decision to avoid dealing with problems that are better left in the past. This doesn't mean you're ignoring issues; rather, it means you're making a conscious decision to go forward by letting go of constraints that are holding you back.

DECEMBER 29

"If right now, in this moment, all you
are left with is yourself, then you will
discover that you have everything you
need and more."

I f right now you realize you can only rely on yourself, that in itself
is a profoundly powerful insight. In your time alone, you will
realize that you already possess all the skills, knowledge, and abilities
that will help you succeed. You will find more than just enough; you
will find an abundance of inner richness that can aid you on your
path to discovery, love, peace, and fulfillment.

DECEMBER 30

"It ended so that you could love
yourself better. It ended so that you
could see that there was something
more for you to receive. It ended
because your heart was meant for
something different. It ended because
you needed more of you. It ended so
that you could remember who you
were before you gave your heart to
someone who proved to be heartless."

The end of the relationship was not a chance event but rather a
way to learn to love and understand yourself better. It ended
so you could see that you could have more rewarding experiences
and relationships in the future. The ending meant that your heart
was meant to love someone else, maybe someone better. It made you
think about yourself and understand that you needed to give yourself
more love and attention. Most importantly, it was the start of a
journey to find yourself again, a journey that takes you back to the
person you were before you loved someone who didn't love you back
the way you deserved.

DECEMBER 31

"The same strength you used to hold on tight to the person who hurt you with hopes of them changing is the same strength you'll use to let go and move forward into spaces that are not built to hold the people who have chosen to treat you like shit."

Your inner strength can be seen in how you stubbornly clung to someone who had brought you harm in the hopes that they would eventually change. The strength you use to cling to relationships that don't fulfill you can also be used to break free of them and go on with your life. It's the strength you'll need to venture into uncharted territories in life, ones where you'll be treated with the respect, love, and positivity you deserve rather than with the negativity of those who have opted to mistreat you.

As the year comes to an end, I want to reach out to everyone who has gone through the pain and sadness of a hard breakup. It's been a year of facing problems, feeling sad, and maybe even getting lost at times. But remember that every sunset is followed by a sunrise, every end is a new start, and every goodbye brings the promise of a new hello.

In the past year, you've probably found out you have strengths you didn't know you had, felt feelings you didn't think you'd feel, and walked down roads you never planned to take. Even though these things hurt, they have helped you become more resilient and grow as a person. Your journey through the pain shows how brave, flexible, and strong you are.

Let's take a moment to think about how important ends are. They are not signs of failure but rather things that make us want to change and move on to new episodes. Each ending makes room for a new beginning, a better experience, and a better knowledge of oneself. As you enter the New Year, take with you the lessons you've learned from the events you've been through, and know that you are now better prepared to deal with whatever the future may bring.

May the coming year be a time for you to start over and find yourself again. Accept the person you've become, which is shaped by the struggles you've faced and overcome, and be proud of your journey of healing and getting to know yourself. Be open to the new, the surprising, and the exciting things that are just around the corner.

I want to encourage you to keep growing the love you have for yourself in the New Year. Your heart is strong and can love more than you can imagine. It deserves to be loved by others and, most of all, by you. Don't forget that the strength you used to get through the storm is the same strength that will get you to better weather.

So, here's to you, your strength and courage, and the wonderful new starts that the coming year will bring. Remember that you're not just staying alive; you're changing, and every step you take brings you closer to a better, more positive future. Take this word of hope into the New Year: You haven't just survived; you've grown, and the best is yet to come.

NOTES

r.h. Sin